How To Transform Your Life

Six Steps To Lasting Happiness

How To Transform Your Life

Six Steps To Lasting Happiness

by

Barbara Goosen Shelby

1stBooks-rev. 9/12/00

ABOUT THE BOOK

This simple, yet profound, method teaches you how to:

* **Open up the lines of supply to abundance and happiness.**
* **Know what to do with negative emotions.**
* **Learn how to relate to others in a loving manner.**
* **Allow your life to flow as effortlessly as possible.**
* **Take care of yourself & still keep a spiritual focus**
* **Use forgiveness as a tool to help yourself.**

"After an extremely abusive childhood, 'turning over to the Source' was frightening, but doing so has led to a wonderful strength and feeling of companionship. An amazing sense of safekeeping and joy is now a part of my daily life, thanks to the Six Step Method."

Allyson A. Barrett,
Dental Researcher,
University of Florida

"We all know anger kills--the spirit, relationships, happiness. Insights from HOW TO TRANSFORM YOUR LIFE have delighted many people I have counseled, both individually and in workshops, and helped them attain peace."

Mary Bergan Blanchard,
M.Ed, LPC,
Albuquerque, New Mexico

"I'm very thankful that I became involved with Barbara Shelby's method of reconnection to the Source. Through practicing the Six Steps, I have found new awareness, appreciation, and gratitude for the synchronicity of life, for the gifts and opportunities in each situation I face, and for the freedom of letting go of the specific outcomes that I cannot control anyway."

Marty M. Peters, Ph.D.,
Director, Academic Achievement Program,
College of Law, University of Iowa

"Since I began practicing the Six Steps four years ago, I have seen major improvements in my work, my relationships, my physical health, and my mental attitude. Most importantly, the Source has become a vibrant, on-going Presence in my life. Don't be deceived by the simplicity of the approach; it can bring profound, life-transforming benefits!"

Susan Tiano, Ph.D.,
Professor and Chair of Sociology,
University of New Mexico

"I recently had a remarkable experience using the Six-Step Method. I wanted to focus my mind by repeating a mantra over and over. I used the breath meditation from Chapter Three of HOW TO TRANSFORM YOUR LIFE, with amazing results. Ten days later, two consulting job offers appeared, unsolicited. Both were perfect for my needs and both materialized on the same day!"

Peter Pretorius, M.S. in Instructional Systems,
Curriculum Designer,
Revere, Massachusetts

*This book is lovingly dedicated to Jared,
without whose wisdom and patience
it could not have been written.*

Please note that all names within the text
have been changed to protect the identities of those
who have been willing to share their experiences.

FOREWORD

By April O'Connell, Ph.D.
NOVA Southeastern University, Santa Fe Community College

WHY WRITE A FOREWORD?

A foreword to a book has several purposes. First, it is generally written by someone who is knowledgeable in the subject matter and who can verify its contents. Second, a foreword is supposed to state why the book would be helpful to the reader.

CAN I VERIFY THE CONTENTS OF THIS BOOK?

I have been a professor of psychology, teaching classes about personal growth and development for more than 35 years. I am also the author of two textbooks in this area. As a professional in the field, I can assure you that the themes you will find in HOW TO TRANSFORM YOUR LIFE—SIX STEPS TO LASTING HAPPINESS (such as the theme that we can be happy if we *choose* to be happy) are in keeping with today's holistic understanding of health and growth. The Six Steps are in keeping with some of the most dynamic work being done today in the health-related and mental health-related professions.

WOULD READING THIS BOOK BE HELPFUL?

Since this question is highly personal, the only way I can respond is to share with you my own personal experience in practicing this transformational Method.

I first met Barbara Goosen Shelby on New Year's Eve, 1989. It was a crucial meeting. I was in one of the lowest psychological and physical depressions of my life, the result of several catastrophic events of the preceding year. Even though I didn't know it then, such events would continue for the next two years. Some of the catastrophes included a long, drawn-out divorce; a mountain of debts for which I was legally (but not morally or ethically) responsible; and the deaths of two adult children. I was having difficulty keeping up with my expenses, let alone paying off my debts. To prevent bankruptcy, I began teaching in a second college on weekends and evenings, in addition to my already full-time college position. All of this began to take its toll on my emotional and physical health.

As I think back over those years, I am filled with a sense of wonder and gratitude that Barbara Shelby came into my life just at that time. Using the healing method presented in this book, I was able to work through most of the grief, guilt, and despair I had been feeling. Gradually I began to recover from the chronic disease that had overtaken me. Had it not been for the healing effects of the Six-Step Method of transformation presented in this book, I might today be confined to a wheel chair, as some victims of my illness are five and ten years after diagnosis.

I will not pretend this was my only treatment. I have always been holistic in my approach to my mental and physical health and have practiced healthful techniques and habits. But I can affirm that the transformational method of healing you'll find in this book was a major source of my getting well again—mentally, emotionally, physically, and, yes, spiritually.

Research studies of the last several decades all support the holistic concept that every dimension of our existence affects every other dimension of our lives. Change your attitude, and your perception of the world will change. As your world view changes, so will your emotions change. And as your emotions change, so will your physical health.

HOW TO TRANSFORM YOUR LIFE—SIX STEPS TO LASTING HAPPINESS contains a powerful technique that can greatly benefit anyone's physical, mental, emotional, and spiritual growth. I hope that what I have just written will encourage you to read this book. More than that, I hope you will work with the transformational Method described in the following pages.

Try it, practice it. You don't have to be a "true believer." Work with the Six Steps. Observe yourself. Collect data. Record your experiences and observations. Notice your bodily symptoms and changes in your health. Record your thoughts and feelings and notice the improvement in your everyday relationships. Be aware of your spiritual growth and how your personal world is being transformed day by day. Make the Six Steps a part of your life.

Watch with pleasure as your new "inner" experiences bring you closer to your true self, and make you more creative and more integrated in your "outer" world of family, friends, and work relationships. If you truly practice the Six-Step Method detailed in this book, all of this can happen to you in a relatively short time. It's one of the best investments of time and effort that you will ever make.

WHAT THIS BOOK CAN DO FOR YOU

By Barbara Goosen Shelby

There seems to be too much pain in the world. We're bombarded with it—in the newspapers, on radio and T.V., in movies, books and conversation. Not only that, but as we grow older, we become more and more aware that we, ourselves, are often in pain. Our plans don't work out, our relationships fall apart, our jobs don't satisfy us, our hopes and dreams keep drifting farther and farther out of reach.

Sometimes we're so overwhelmed by the enormity of all the pain — the rest of the world's and our own — that we just want to shut it out. When we can't shut it out, we want to scream, "Somebody, *do* something!" The trouble is, what can be done about such a massive problem? And who is the "somebody" who can do it?

The solution is, I think, much simpler than it seems. The main thing to understand is that dealing with the world's pain doesn't mean pulling off some grandiose scheme which will change the face of the planet overnight. And relieving your own misery and suffering doesn't require a fairy godmother or a magic lamp.

The only magic you really need is the willingness to accept the fact that *you* are the "somebody" who can solve the problem. This willingness opens up for you an incredible power to change your life so that you are no longer a slave to misery and suffering, whatever forms those take for you. And as you shift your own life to become happier and more peaceful, you can't help shifting the world around you. Changes will begin to take place in your daily life and in your personal world in ways you've never even dreamed possible. The effects of that can't help rippling out to influence the greater world beyond it.

Once you set this energy in motion, it seems to take on a life of its own. This doesn't mean, of course, that you don't have to do your part, because you do. What is your part? Simply to put into practice the Six-Step method detailed in this book. This method has been tested over many years and found to work in amazing ways. The Six Steps help you reconnect to the Source of All Good, whether you call it God, Christ, Buddha, Allah, the Great Spirit, the Universe, or any other name. Practicing these Steps daily will open up that Source energy and make it consistently available to you.

You may be "religious," or not—it doesn't matter. You can still access this energy and receive its help, simply by practicing the Steps on a regular basis. Remember, we're talking here about *spiritual* help. "Religious" and "spiritual" are not always the same thing. You don't have to be religious to be spiritual, or to make this spiritual connection and receive the benefit from it. "Spiritual" really means "of the spirit," and almost everyone agrees that there is something, some essence which is uniquely oneself, which reaches beyond the mere physical. What you call it doesn't really matter. What you do about reconnecting to it does.

You don't have to believe in the God of those around you, or the religious teachings you grew up with to be truly spiritual in your focus. I, myself, was raised in a very rigid church which spoke outwardly of God's love and caring. Yet underneath that surface was a bedrock of fear and punishment, even hatred. For many years I rebelled against such a deity and felt adrift on a sea of uncertainty and unhappiness. Only when I was introduced to the Six Steps and began to practice them, did my life shift for the better. Since then, I've realized the tremendous importance of these Steps, of how they can reconnect a person to his or her inner truth and power. I've seen the truly miraculous way they can work in the lives of those who apply them. Some people have even discovered a deeper and clearer understanding of their own religious beliefs through practicing the Steps.

If you make these Six Steps an active part of your life, they *will* work, they *will* transform your life. You can test this out for yourself. All it should take is thirty days of dedicated practice. I have yet to find someone who really made a commitment to working the Steps daily for this period who did not experience results.

The discussion of the Six Steps begins in full in Chapter 3. I hope you'll also read the first and second chapters carefully, because they give you a firm foundation for understanding how and why the Steps work.

In making a commitment to practice the Six Steps for thirty days, you give yourself the opportunity to change your life in a positive way forever. You become a winner in every way, because the only thing you can possibly lose is your pain.

And you'll even be doing your part to help the world!

CHAPTER 1

HOW TO GET WHAT YOU REALLY WANT

"Sometimes we get so caught up in the drama of our lives that we forget what's truly important."

"I JUST WANT TO BE HAPPY!"

What do you really want from life? Success? Money? A loving relationship? Spiritual growth? Peace of mind? Most of us struggle to accumulate as many items on this list as we can. We spend years trying to "get ahead"— to own more, make more money, accomplish more, be more important, be better liked, get bigger promotions, be more spiritually focused. We do this because we believe these things will finally bring us what we *really* want — happiness.

Don't we always want what we want — whether it's a good feeling or a new car or a better job—because we believe that it will make us happy?

We spend weeks, months, even years, frantically pushing to have more, do more, be more. We hope that if we struggle long enough and hard enough, some day, somehow we'll finally be happy. But if happiness is our true goal, why is it so hard for us to just focus on that?

Why do we have the idea that happiness only comes as a result of achieving other goals, instead of understanding that happiness is a legitimate goal in itself?

HAPPINESS IS A LEGITIMATE GOAL, NOT JUST A SIDE EFFECT

Most of us are taught very early that being happy is something which finally (and automatically) happens when we at last get what we've worked so hard for—the house, the money, the job, the relationship, the education, the spiritual focus. The fact that the majority of the people who have devoted their lives to this struggle *don't* feel happy and fulfilled when they finally "arrive" seems to have very little effect on this belief. We look at the big income, the mansion, the cars, the expensive clothes, and overlook the unhappy relationships, broken marriages and estranged children and friends.

Happiness is the carrot dangling on the end of the stick. What we ignore is the fact that the carrot will always continue to be just out of reach, no matter how long or how far we push toward it. But if happiness is a legitimate goal, not just a carrot on a stick, not just "pie in the sky" to entice us to work harder, how do we accomplish it? The answer to this question is so simple that we usually overlook it.

We reach the goal of happiness by *choosing* to be happy.

"What do you mean, *choose* to be happy?", I can almost hear you demanding. Because surely, if it were that easy, we'd all be happy right now, wouldn't we? Unfortunately, it isn't as easy as it sounds. I did say it was simple, but "simple" and "easy" aren't always the same thing.

By choosing to be happy, I mean choosing to do those things which help us let go of *un*happiness. This includes, among other things, letting go of our fears, dealing with our anger in healthy ways, and refusing to judge situations and people negatively. It means focusing on those things which make happiness a part of our daily lives. Being happy on a daily basis *is,* indeed, a choice. But making that choice in a conscious way takes some effort on our part. And not only effort, but the willingness to make that effort day after day after day.

WE CONSTANTLY CHOOSE

Life is a shifting fabric of choices. Every action we take is the result of a choice we've made, whether we're aware of it or not. Once in a while we notice we're choosing, but usually our choices are unconscious and automatic.

But we do choose, from the smallest action to the largest—when we'll get up, where we'll go, what we'll wear, what we'll do. We choose how we'll respond to the ringing phone, whether we'll have potatoes or rice for dinner, whether to cut short one activity to take care of something else. Even deciding not to choose is a choice.

And, in spite of what most of us have been taught, what we think and feel is also a choice.

You may want to protest, "Wait a minute, that's ridiculous! I *might* agree that I choose a lot of my actions, but I draw the line at saying that what I think or feel is a choice! My thoughts just come, and when things happen, I just feel how I feel. I don't have any control over that."

I agree with you that thoughts and feelings seem to "just come". It can take only an instant for a thought to be there in our minds, or for a feeling to overwhelm us. Where choice enters in is *after we have the thought or feeling*. Obviously we don't consciously choose whether or not we'll allow the feeling or the thought to come—it's already there.

What we do choose is how we'll react to it.

No one is ever obligated to keep a feeling that isn't truly wanted, or a thought that leads to unhappiness. We are always free to choose positive thoughts and feelings and to let go of negative ones. Which thoughts and feelings we choose is extremely important, because what we think and feel determines what we do.

CHOOSE *FOR* YOURSELF, INSTEAD OF *AGAINST* YOURSELF

Choosing which thoughts and feelings to keep and which to let go of, may at first strike you as impossible. Actually it isn't as difficult as it might seem. All you need to do is be willing to test the idea. You'll want to give yourself a fair trial period, say a month, of really working at it. **Really working at it means making an effort to pay attention to what you're thinking and feeling on a moment-to-moment basis.**

This may take a little practice. Usually we human beings only notice the end results of our thoughts and feelings, and then only after these become so uncomfortable that we can't ignore them any longer. So, in order to choose *for* yourself, you'll have to give yourself permission to begin noticing what you think and feel *as* you're doing it. You'll also need to pay attention to the choices you make as a result of your thoughts or feelings.

WHAT YOU DO IS A RESULT OF WHAT YOU THINK AND FEEL

As you watch what's happening, you'll begin to connect your actions with the choices you've made. You'll also become more and more aware that those choices are the result of whether you kept or let go of certain thoughts and feelings.

Paying attention like this may seem a bit overwhelming at first. Most of us are used to just letting life happen and then wondering why it happened as it did. Noticing what we do with

4

our thoughts and feelings puts us more in touch with the inner mechanics of our lives. Being more aware also opens the door to being able to choose happiness over unhappiness.

When you pay attention to what's going on with your thoughts and feelings, you're better able to decide which ideas and emotions you want to keep, and which you want to let go of. To make the process of being aware easier, you can keep a journal, or notebook, in which you write down what you're noticing about your thoughts, feelings, and choices. You can just jot down brief notes as things happen, to remind you of what's going on. Later, you can combine these notes with your Six Step Notebook, which we'll discuss in Chapter 11. Or you can make your awareness observations a separate record.

FOCUS IS EVERYTHING

Your focus is how you look at things, how you view what is happening to you and around you. Your choices create your focus. Often other people's behavior, or outside circumstances and events, seem to dictate what our focus will be. If someone suggests that we're looking at a certain situation in a less than useful way, we may feel irritated. "Well, how else can I look at it?" we snap. We see the suggestion as a stupid comment about an upsetting situation we feel powerless to change.

Keeping in mind that our choices create our focus, how else *could* we look at a situation we don't like?

SHIFT YOUR FOCUS TO CHANGE YOUR EXPERIENCE

Often we believe that a situation is simply what it is, that choosing to see it differently can't change it. But is it possible that events and circumstances only *seem* to be a certain way? Furthermore, could the way they *seem* depend upon how we choose to view them?

Studies show that five different persons witnessing the same accident will usually give five different versions of what happened. And three people undergoing exactly the same difficult circumstances may have three completely different experiences. One just barely survives and never really recovers. The second struggles through, but is scarred for life. The third looks at the situation and says, "Well, I certainly wish this weren't happening, but let me see what it is that I need to learn from it." This person may end up feeling that the experience was the most valuable of the entire lifetime. The only difference between the three is their focus, how they choose to view what happened to them.

So, how one person sees or understands an event can be very different from the way someone else does. How can that happen? If events or circumstances are really only what they are, this shouldn't be possible. But what if events and circumstance are somehow influenced just by the fact that we witness or are involved in them?

Certain scientific observations suggest that an experiment is actually influenced by the attention of the person conducting, or even by someone simply viewing, that experiment. This gives us even more reason to believe that how we see things *does* influence what they become for us.

WHAT WE SEE IS WHAT WE GET

If you're old enough, you may remember Flip Wilson's character, Geraldine, whose stock phrase was "What you see is what you get!" That statement is not just a funny line. It seems increasingly true that what we see (our focus) creates what we get (what the situation becomes for us).

In other words, *our focus (how we view things) creates our experience.*

Put all this together with the fact that we always choose, and you can see that we also choose our focus, or how we'll view a situation or event.

YOUR FOCUS CREATES YOUR EXPERIENCE

How does this principle work?

Let's say your boss chews you out for no good reason. You have a choice as to how you'll react to this injustice. You can become upset and lose your temper and yell back. Or you can realize that there must be something bothering your boss which is causing this behavior. If you're willing to choose *not* to allow yourself to become overly distressed, your boss can be angry, while you remain calm and in control of your reactions.

It's important to understand that the usual way of responding, which is to get upset, is often based on a feeling of "righteous anger." ("How dare he/she talk to me that way! It just isn't fair. That makes me so mad!") Righteous anger is one of the trickiest emotions we human beings feel.

Righteous anger is really plain old rage, often buried inside us since childhood. This rage stems from the hurt feelings and helplessness we may have felt as children. It disguises itself, however, as something that anybody in his right mind would be certain to feel in this situation. It seems completely justified, because surely only a wimp would swallow such an injustice.

Righteous anger is mostly old, repressed childhood feelings of injustice and powerlessness. It doesn't really fit with our adult behavior, and it's very good at getting us into trouble.

In a sense, then, your boss's behavior isn't even the true cause of your righteous anger. You're really furious at your parents, brother, sister, teacher, or someone else from the past. It wasn't safe to show your anger toward them when you first felt it, so you stuffed it down inside. Your boss's behavior has suddenly brought up those old, bad feelings.

7

You may not be able to avoid *feeling* angry, as an immediate reaction, but you *can* choose to let go of the anger as soon as you realize you're feeling it. In other words, you can deliberately choose a focus which allows you to remain peaceful. Or you can choose a focus ruled by the anger which has surged up inside you. The anger is then in control. This almost always causes pain and sometimes leads to disaster.

Keeping anger only leads to more anger, both yours and your boss's. It may even stir up strong feelings in those around you, who then take sides. This causes worse distress, feelings of separation, and could lead to the loss of your job. Letting go of the anger relieves much of your stress, opening up your ability to feel happier and allowing your boss and everyone else involved to calm down more easily. Even if you feel you need to take certain steps to protect your rights and to stand up for yourself, you'll be able to do that from a position of strength, rather than of weakness.

You can see that if you choose the focus of anger, you create one kind of experience for yourself. If, on the other hand, you choose to let the anger go and focus on being more understanding and peaceful, you offer yourself a completely different kind of experience.

In addition, choosing to be more understanding and peaceful settles and stabilizes you. Releasing your anger also creates an atmosphere which allows things to become balanced more easily and quickly. It recognizes each person's value as a human being and allows for the fact that human beings often make mistakes. So, the next time you feel a surge of righteous anger, remind yourself that you can choose what you'll do with it. If you choose to let the anger go and create a more loving, peaceful, satisfying experience, you choose to react from a position of strength. You choose *for* yourself, instead of *against* yourself.

(We'll talk more about reasons for keeping or letting anger go and how to stay peaceful and still not be a doormat in Chapter 5.)

FOCUS ON THE POSITIVE, NOT THE NEGATIVE

If our focus makes life what it becomes for us, it's easy to see what we need to do. **We have to begin to see things in a more positive way, if we want life to be happier.**

I have a cousin who used to send us long, cheerful letters when I was growing up. My family was unhappy much of the time, so of course my own focus then wasn't a particularly positive one. (We usually learn our focus as children from the adults around us.) When my mother would read this cousin's letters aloud, I used to think, "What a Pollyanna! Nobody could be that happy all the time!" It actually made me feel angry at her. (How dare she be happy when we weren't!)

After I grew up and got to know this cousin better, I realized that her life had been touched by as many problems and sorrows as anyone else's. She just handled these issues by choosing to see all the good possible in each situation. She certainly wasn't happy every minute of every day, not was she avoiding reality. She simply refused to "get into" the misery when something happened which she didn't prefer. Her focus was on the positive things in her life. This positive focus helped her to deal with those circumstances which appeared negative more easily than if she had allowed feelings of gloom and doom to overtake her.

APPEARANCES AREN'T ALWAYS WHAT THEY SEEM

Notice that last sentence says "events and circumstances which *appeared* negative." Things can and do happen which seem very negative. We often label these events and circumstances "bad" because they remind us of old pain, or they don't fit what we expected or believe we want.

We also may view what's happening as bad because we hardly ever understand what's *really* going on while an event is taking place. We *think* we know what's taking place, but we don't. We don't really know, because we can't. We aren't able to fully understand what's going on in any situation while it's happening. There are too many things under the surface and behind the scenes about which we have no clue.

Only when we look back on an event can we more easily sort out what really went on, and why. And sometimes we can't even do that. This can make us feel very confused, insecure and afraid. In order to feel safer and less confused, we need to understand certain basic principles that govern life. When we're aware of the ground rules, it's easier to make choices which allow us to use these precepts to help, rather than hinder, ourselves. In Chapter 2 we'll discuss these principles and see how they form the foundation for the Six Steps.

REMINDERS FROM CHAPT.

1. Happiness is a legitimate goal, in and of itself.
2. We become happy by choosing to be happy.
3. What we do is always based on the choices that grow out of what we think and feel.
4. How we see things (what our focus is) influences what they become for us. Our focus creates our experience of life.
5. We always choose our focus.
6. "Righteous" anger comes out of the past. It never helps us, and often gets us in trouble.
7. We have to begin to view things in a more positive, cheerful way, if we want life to be happier.
8. Appearances aren't always what they seem.
9. In order to feel safer and less confused, we need to understand certain basic principles that govern life, and learn to use them for our benefit.

CHAPTER 2

THE FOUR BASIC PRINCIPLES AND THE SIX STEPS

"The Six Steps helped me begin the process of finding peace in my soul and love in my heart."

I COULD DO BETTER, IF I JUST KNEW THE GROUND RULES!

How often have you felt that life certainly would be easier if you'd arrived with an instruction kit? Life, however, doesn't work like that. Each of us has to find our own way. And sometimes it isn't easy.

Fortunately, there are certain time-tested principles which *can* help us. Over the centuries, these have been used by many people with great success. They still work today and can show us how to live more happily and successfully. We just have to be willing to put them into practice.

YOU CAN'T DO IT ALL YOURSELF

One of the most important principles is that you can't do it all yourself.

"Oh great", you may be thinking. "What does that mean? You've just said my experience depends on my focus, and *I'm* responsible for choosing that, along with my thoughts and feelings. So what's this 'I can't do it all myself' stuff!"

'You can't do it all yourself' simply means that you're human. Being human means you have neither the foresight nor the insight to understand everything in your life. It also means you're mostly unaware of all the possible and probable outcomes of any given situation. There are too many things going on at too many different levels for you to be able to understand everything.

Fortunately, you're not required to understand everything. (In fact, it's even possible that you're not *supposed* to—at least, not entirely.) And regardless of how much you can or can't understand, you *do* have help. This help is always available, twenty-four hours a day, seven days a week. You don't need a phone or a fax to tap into it, and its cost is very reasonable. All you need to invest is some time and effort.

MEET YOUR BUSINESS PARTNER

The help I'm talking about can actually be thought of as a business partnership. Because whether you work inside or outside your home, you are in business for yourself. That business is your life.

Your life *has* to be a partnership because "you can't do it all yourself." This principle means that you can't adequately run your life all alone. There are too many unknowns involved, too many factors over which you have little or no direct control.

Fortunately, your business partner isn't hindered by the many blocks and inadequacies from which you, as a human being, suffer. As you may have already guessed, your partner in this business of life is the universal energy most refer to as "God", or your "Higher Power." Call it whatever you like— Source, God, Christ, Buddha, Allah, Great Spirit, Universal Power, Higher Power—it really doesn't matter. For the purposes of this book, I will use the term, "the Source of All Good," or simply, "the Source."

GAIN CONTROL OF YOUR LIFE BY LETTING GO

You can think of yourself as having about a fifteen percent capacity to conduct your life well, and your Partner, the Source, as being in charge of the other eighty-five percent. This means that, no matter how hard you try, you aren't going to be able to really run your life smoothly unless you tap into your Partner's greater ability.

For those of us who have a need to feel in control, this may sound pretty scary. Actually, it can be a great relief when we realize that we don't *have* to do it all. There is a part of us, the Source part, which knows exactly what to do and how to do it, if only we give our permission.

And permission is necessary. Our Partner, the Source, will never force help on us, because that would tamper with our free will. We have to be willing to do those things which allow the Source to assist us fully, without violating our free will, in order to receive that help.

It is a paradox, but the only way we can ever fully gain control of our lives is by turning over the control to that part of us (the Source part) which knows what to do with it.

Our modest fifteen percent of the business of life really consists of doing those things which keep us connected to the Source, so that It is free to take care of everything else.

The thought of having only fifteen percent control over your life may, for a moment, make you feel helpless and vulnerable. If you think about what this really means, however, you can see that everything you need for a happy and fulfilling life is available through a willing partnership with the universal energy, the Source. And once you begin to work in partnership with that Source connection inside you, you can accomplish virtually anything.

WHAT YOU SEND OUT COMES BACK MULTIPLIED

One very effective way of taking care of your fifteen percent is to practice the Six Steps described in this book. Before we explain the Six Steps in detail, however, let's complete our discussion of the four basic principles which govern our lives. We've already talked about the first two: "What we see is what we get", and "We can't do it all ourselves." The third principle is one most of us seldom, if ever, think about, but it is constantly at work in our lives.

This third principle, "What you send out comes back multiplied," means that whenever you "send out" the expectation of certain results from your actions, you draw back circumstances which fit that expectation. These also reinforce your feelings and beliefs. If you are constantly sending out dissatisfaction and unhappiness, you soon attract enough negative experiences to "prove" that people and situations, even life, itself, hold only misery for you. This becomes a vicious circle, because every time you send out negative feelings, you attract experiences which seem to justify your pessimism. Then you can say, "See, I knew it wouldn't work!" Or, "See, people really *are* rotten. Just look how that person treated me!" Or, "Why does everything have to happen to me?"

"What you send out comes back multiplied" means that you can, indeed, "prove" to yourself that almost anything is true. Hard as it may be to accept, you will basically receive whatever you choose to attract into your life through your focus and your expectations. This doesn't, of course, mean that every "negative" event that takes place is only the result of your outlook. All kinds of things happen to everyone. Separation, sadness, even death are all a part of life. The important thing is how you view and respond to what happens. Even if circumstances are not what you would prefer them to be, your willingness to be as positively focused as possible will draw new, more positive experiences to you.

BELIEVING HELPS TO MAKE IT SO

Whatever you draw to you returns, ultimately, as the result of what you have chosen to send out. If you want positive results, you must choose to send out energy based on the belief that people and life are basically good. This energy will then bring back experiences of good which reinforce your belief.

Of course, choosing to believe that life is basically positive doesn't mean that every person you meet will always be a bearer of sweetness and light. Everybody has their "off" moments, even the most determined optimist. And those people who have chosen to view life negatively will tend to be grumpy. However, you will generally find that most people try to be friendly and helpful.

This fits right in with the first principle, discussed in Chapter One, that "what we see is what we get." If you choose to see the good in people and situations, then you will receive good in return. And if you send out your belief that life is basically rewarding, despite the frustrations we all run up against at times, this draws rewarding experiences to you on a continuing basis.

But what about the "bad" things that sometimes happen? The fourth basic principle deals with this undeniable part of life.

WHAT YOU RESIST, YOU LOCK IN PLACE

You may think that this principle doesn't make sense, but see if the following story helps you understand it better.

You're walking along a path in a forest, making pretty good progress. Oh, here and there you find a pothole or a detour, but on the whole you're doing very well. Suddenly, straight ahead, is a twelve foot high brick wall that extends as far as you can see on either side. Now what do you do?

You have three choices. One is to be so overwhelmed by the height and extent of the wall that you just sink down beside it and give up. Some of us do that. The second choice is the most common one. You become angry and indignant. How dare this wall be here in the way! It isn't fair! Why does everything have to happen to me? You may pound your fists, or even your head, on the wall in frustration.

The problem is that you can stand there forever, beating your head and fists against the bricks. It won't make a bit of difference to the wall. It isn't going to move the wall, even a fraction of an inch. All you'll do is end up with sore fists and a terrible headache.

The third choice is by far the best. You can have a temper tantrum first, and get it out of your system, if you want. Then calm yourself and sit down at the foot of the wall. Relax.

Acknowledge to yourself that you definitely don't like having the wall there.

Let yourself accept the fact that **it's impossible to fight what is, and win**. And this wall definitely IS. Your not wanting it to be is not going to make it go away. In other words, **let go of your resistance to the way things are at the moment**. The wall IS, and you can't fight that fact unless you want to waste your time and energy. Instead, *let the situation be what it is and, for the moment (because you really have no other useful choice), let that be O.K.!*

This does *not* mean that you are saying it's wonderful and you love it and want it to stay that way forever. It does mean that you are willing to stop exhausting your time and energy in a losing battle. Instead, you are willing to give yourself the space to see what needs to be done next, so you can get past this apparent block.

Withdrawing your resistance to the fact that the wall is there allows you to look around and notice what you couldn't see before. Maybe you discover a log that you can prop against the wall. Then you can climb up, get over the top, and move on. Or, you may see some loose mortar between the bricks. All it will take is a sharp rock to dig with, and soon you'll have a hole large enough to crawl through.

But neither of these, nor any other option, is available to you if all your time and energy is being used to beat your head on the wall!

RELAX AND ALLOW

Here's another illustration of how the principle of "what you resist you lock in place" works. Suppose all the good things you want from life are gathered together in one room. You've been

18

told to relax and allow your good to come to you, but you really want to get at it, so you push and push against the door, trying to force your way in. The harder you push, however, the tighter the door seems to stick. What you haven't taken into account is the fact that this particular door opens *outward!* You can push forever, and you won't be able to get at what you want. Instead, you have to be willing to acknowledge that the setup isn't the way you thought it *should* be. Once you simply let it be the way it is, you can relax, step back, and allow the door to open.

Letting go of resistance in order to get things to open up and shift is one of the most difficult principles to understand and accept. Human beings have a hard time allowing something which they don't prefer to just be the way it is and for the moment, at least, letting the way it is be O.K. Instead, we want to shout, "But it's *not* O.K.! How can I possibly say that it is?"

We have to understand that, if we want the situation to improve, it *has* to be O.K.— at least for the moment. We can't fight what is, and win. Withdrawing our resistance actually unlocks the way things are, so they *can* shift and improve.

It's really a matter of applying the principle so that it works *for* us, instead of against us. If we resist how things are, we waste precious time and energy beating our heads against whatever wall we happen to be facing. Then we wonder why we feel so frustrated and why everything seems stuck. (If this is still a difficult concept to accept, read the discussion of Step Five, in Chapter 8.)

THE FOUR BASIC PRINCIPLES OF LIFE

That is the fourth and last of the rules which govern our lives. When we understand and accept these four Basic

Principles, we can begin to make them work for us, instead of against us. Here they are again, listed in order.

1. **What you "see" is what you get.**
   (Focus is everything.)
2. **You can't do it all yourself.**
   (You need help, which is available.)
3. **What you send out comes back multiplied.**
   (Your beliefs and behaviors attract your experience and your experience reinforces what you think and do.)
4. **What you resist, you lock in place.**
   (Letting go of your resistance allows things to open up and shift for the better.)

The best way we can use these Principles to help ourselves is by getting in touch with the universal power which created them. The Source wants very much to help us live our lives more happily and will do just that, if we permit. The Six Steps which follow are certainly not the only way to get in touch with our inner Source power, but they are ones which definitely work.

Regardless of what your individual spiritual beliefs happen to be, you can make good use of the help these Six Steps provide. They do not belong to just one belief system. And don't let yourself get sidetracked or "turned off" by the words used to describe this help. If you don't like the words I've chosen, substitute ones which make more sense to you and make you feel comfortable. Then study the Six Steps and put them into practice. You'll be amazed at the results you'll see!

Here, then, are the tools which will help you connect to the Source, so that It is free to help you. Remember that their practice must be an ongoing process, a daily habit like brushing your teeth or washing your face. You must be willing to work with the Steps, even when you think you'd rather not, to get the results you want. But if you practice them seriously, they will transform your life.

THE SIX STEPS TO LASTING HAPP'

1. **Put your focus where it does the most** '
2. **Ask for what you wish, but ask withou**
3. **Let go of your negative emotions.**
4. **Focus in the moment, doing what comes next, as it is presented to you.**
5. **Let go of negative judgment and your resistance to what's happening.**
6. **Notice and give thanks for the good in your life.**

All of these Steps have their foundation in the four Basic Principles we've already discussed in this chapter. Each one is loaded with the power to help you make these Principles work *for* you, instead of *against* you. The following chapters will explain the Steps in detail.

You don't need to be a college graduate or a spiritual guru to succeed. All that's needed is your willingness to invest a relatively small amount of time and energy to practice these Six Steps on a daily basis. At the end of just one month of daily practice, you'll be experiencing results which will make you eager to continue.

REMINDERS FROM CHAPTER 2

1. Understanding the four basic principles makes life easier and happier.
2. Your life is a business partnership with the Source.
3. You only have a fifteen percent capacity to run your life well. The Source has the other eighty-five percent.
4. What you receive is the result of what you have sent out.
5. It's important to understand that you can't fight what is, and win.
6. Withdrawing your resistance actually unlocks the way things are, so they can shift and improve.
7. The best way to use the four Basic Principles is to get in touch with the universal power which created them.
8. The Six Steps help connect you to the Source energy, so It can help you.
9. Practicing these Six Steps as a thirty day commitment will leave you amazed and delighted with the results.

CHAPTER 3

STEP ONE:
PUT YOUR FOCUS
WHERE IT DOES THE MOST GOOD

"As my focus began to change, my beliefs changed, and so did my life."

The following chapters cover what you need to know to put the Six Steps into daily practice. Please remember that working with these Steps is an ongoing process. You can't just do it once, and think things are taken care of. You can't just do it now and then, hit or miss, and expect to see results. You have to be willing to apply the steps on a daily basis for at least a month, as a commitment, in order to receive the benefits you want. Remember, this commitment is really to yourself and to your own happiness. And since your life probably is not always the way you'd like it to be at this present time, you have nothing to lose but your pain.

Here, then, is the explanation of what each Step means and what each one can do for you.

STEP 1. PUT YOUR FOCUS
WHERE IT DOES THE MOST GOOD

We have three basic choices about where we put our focus, or how we look at things.

The first choice is to direct our focus outside ourselves into the "drama" of daily life.

When we do this, we tend to get sucked into other people's feelings and problems. We often end up taking on these problems and feelings and mistaking them for our own. This causes us to try to take care of other people's business, instead of our own. This "drama focus" keeps our priorities confused and often turns us into "busybodies". We become excited by disaster and misery. We forget why we're here and what our real business in life is. Focusing on the outer drama effectively keeps us from doing what we need to do for ourselves to remain physically, emotionally and spiritually balanced.

The second choice is to turn our focus inside ourselves and get it hooked into our own fears, angers, guilts, and other negative emotions.

This makes us self-absorbed and so focused on ourselves and our own problems that we tend to ignore the feelings and rights of others. This intense inner focus causes us to overlook the fact that we are all connected, interwoven with each other like threads in a single tapestry. Intense self-absorption keeps us from relating to others in a balanced manner. We become so caught up in our own problems that our focus grows narrower and narrower, until we end up with emotional and spiritual tunnel vision. This makes us so miserable that hardly anyone wants to be around us for very long.

About now you may be saying, "Wait a minute! This is getting too hard to figure out! How can I see other people as interwoven with me, yet not get caught up in their feelings and problems? How am I supposed to keep from getting tangled up in either their negative "stuff", or my own?

The third choice explains how to deal with that dilemma.

The third choice is to make our focus more inward than outward, but to go past our own emotions to a deeper place within ourselves.

Here, in this deep, inner place, we touch that part of us which is connected to something greater than ourselves, that God/Source part within us. This part is as intimate as our breathing, or the cells that make up our bodies. It is our Partner in the business of life, but never demands that we acknowledge this. Regardless of how long it takes for us to begin to open up that partnership, the Source is always ready and more than willing to help us live our lives more happily.

When we turn our focus toward this inner connection, we become aware of a solid, unchanging core of good within ourselves. This central core of our being, this Source part, *is* the source of everything we need to know and have. Recognizing our connection to it gives us the only true sense of stability we can have in our changing world. No matter how much or how often outer circumstances may tremble and shift, this inner core always anchors us to a solid, unshakable center point

How do you get in touch with this solid inner core of being? Do you have to sit in a closet and meditate constantly, or pray twenty-four hours a day, or become so pious that no one can stand you? Of course not. **You get in touch with your central core, the God/Source within you, by putting your focus where it does the most good.**

Putting your focus where it does the most good means letting yourself be aware that while both the outer and inner dramas can be very exciting and seductive, they are also extremely expensive. You pay for them with your peace of mind and with your mental and physical health. They also cost you the ability to interact with others in a happy, loving way.

Putting your focus where it does the most good means getting in touch with your central core of being. It means understanding that what goes on in the outer drama constantly changes. It also means realizing that you have very little, if any, direct control over these changes, or over the drama itself.

The only real control you have, other than choosing how you will react to this changing drama, comes from within, from the God/Source part inside you.

This deep inner part of you *is* the source of all wisdom, love, power, and healing solutions. This Source is available inside you, and wants to make all of these benefits available to you on a regular basis. If you focus outwardly, into the drama, you turn your back on all the help the Source is waiting to give you. And, because you have free will, the Source is not going to force help on you. You have to be willing to understand that the help is there and then indicate that you want it. (We'll discuss the importance of asking for what you want in more detail in Chapter 4.)

As mentioned in the previous chapter, the Source is like a business partner, the business being your life. As your Partner, It has the ability to help you run your life smoothly and happily. When you focus away from your Partner, you essentially withdraw your permission for It to help you. When you focus inwardly toward It, you automatically give the Source the right to take care of the bulk of your life business, which is really Its share of the partnership.

SHIFTING FOCUS TAKES SOME WORK, BUT YOU CAN DO IT

When you let yourself get caught up in the outer drama, moving away from it toward a more inward focus may take a little time. It's like driving a car in one direction for a while, then deciding you need to be headed another way. You have to slow down, put on the brakes, stop and turn around, then gradually build up speed again in the new direction.

The main thing is to decide that this is really what you want to do, then decide you'll stick to your decision. Also, be patient with yourself. Doing something in one way for a long time creates a habit. It usually takes time, in addition to a strong decision to change, to break that habit and develop a different one to take its place.

Sometimes shifting your focus is difficult because you can't believe that there are any possibilities other than the one you see. Later you may realize that what you thought was the only way to do something was just one possible choice of several. But at the moment, it may seem that there are no other options.

One way to help yourself get around this stuck point is to ask, "What if...?" What if this could happen? What if I did that? What if so and so acted differently? What if I looked at the situation this way, instead of the way I've been looking at it?

Let me give you an example. Several years ago I was living in Florida. I had a very busy practice helping people learn, among other things, how to use the Six Steps. I worked long hours, seven days a week, without a real break. One evening I attended a meeting. As I sat down next to a good friend, I suddenly began to cry.

My friend, who is an excellent therapist, took my arm and we left before the meeting started. As we walked out to the car, she turned to me and said, "Let me ask you something. What if you dropped dead tonight? What would happen to your clients?"

I thought about it for a moment. "I guess they'd find somebody else to help them," I replied slowly.

"That's right," she said, "and you'd be dead."

That simple "what if" jolted me into realizing that it wasn't necessary for me to work myself into the ground. Yes, I was helping a few people, but if I suddenly ceased to be there, they'd find help somewhere else. I immediately started to reduce my hours and take some time for myself. Becoming more balanced didn't happen all at once, and I was frequently tempted to forget and go back to the old pattern. But then I would remind myself to keep my new focus. Gradually my balance between work and relaxation became healthier.

BREAKING A "FOCUS LOCK."

Before that incident, however, it seemed to me that I had no other choice but to do what I was doing. I was caught in a "focus lock."

A focus lock is what happens when we become fixated on the way things seem at the moment.

A focus lock prevents us from seeing that our view of the situation is only one possible view. We have such heavy blinders on that we don't allow ourselves to be aware that there are other ways of looking at what's happening. Instead, we need to envision every event or circumstance as having a 360 degree circumference. Usually we focus on only a single degree at a time. Does the fact that we're not noticing the other 359 degrees mean that they don't exist? Of course not.

You can think of your focus as being like the lens you look through when you get your eyes checked. The doctor has you look through one lens, then clicks another one, slightly different, into place. With each click you are asked, "Is this one better, or this one?" Sometimes the two lenses are so close in focus that you don't notice much variation. But always there is at least a little change, a little fuzzing or clearing of the view. And sometimes the difference is quite noticeable.

Events and circumstances are very much like that. All it takes is a click or two of the lens to give us a slightly (or more than slightly) different view of the situation. And remember that **how you see things makes them what they are for you.** To someone else, the situation may not seem to have changed at all. For you, with your shifted focus, it has become entirely different.

LEARN TO BE AN OBSERVER, AS WELL AS A PARTICIPANT

Another way to unlock your focus is to become an observer, not just a participant, in your life. One of the problems of getting caught up in the outer drama is that you tend to be so sucked in that you forget it *is* drama. The way things seem to be at any given moment appear to be the total reality of the situation. Nothing else seems possible. In fact, you usually don't even wonder if anything else *is* possible. This limits your ability to see that any other focus exists, to say nothing of being able to shift your present focus to a more workable one.

The best way to get around this aspect of focus lock is to remember that we all have an inner part, connected to our Source part, which *is* simply an observer. This observer part of us doesn't get caught in the emotions of the drama. It doesn't worry. It doesn't pull old pain and fears out of the past. It doesn't project them into the future. All it does is stand at our shoulder and watch.

Once you become aware of this observer part, you can let it work for you as much of the time as possible. Your observer keeps you aware that the drama *is* drama, not the only reality that exists. Your observer allows you to move back a step or two from your intense involvement in the drama, to be "in the world, but not of it." Your observer helps you remember that focus is a choice. If your present focus isn't producing results you like, you can change the results by shifting your focus.

Do you remember the somewhat smug saying, "You've made your bed—now you have to lie in it"? (I say "smug" because often the speaker sounds a bit pleased that someone else has gotten into an uncomfortable situation.) I frankly prefer this different version:

"If you've made your bed and don't like it, don't lie in it; get up and change the sheets!"

Changing your mental sheets may require some work, but it's worth every ounce of time and energy you invest. Just lying there, in a manner of speaking, and being unhappy with the way things are may seem easier, at least at first. But gradually you become more and more caught in the drama and more and more unhappy. Even if shifting focus causes a little discomfort and extra effort at the beginning, in the end you'll be glad you did it. Your observer can help you choose a useful focus by giving you insight into what's really going on in a particular situation.

For example, when someone is reacting negatively to you (sulking, arguing, yelling, fighting, saying cruel things, etc.), your observer can help you remember to temporarily suspend your judgment and ask yourself two important questions.

The first question to ask yourself when someone gives you a hard time is: "What does this person perceive as a threat in this situation?"

The second question is: "How old is the part of myself who is getting upset?

Once you start asking yourself these two key questions, you begin to realize that other people don't act nasty or unkind for no reason at all. There's always some underlying cause which prompts their behavior, whether or not it makes complete sense to you. You also begin to understand that your own negative reaction is probably not coming from the adult part of you. It's coming from an unhealed child part which is frightened and angered by the other person's behavior.

Understanding these two aspects of the situation puts you more in control of yourself and your responses. You no longer have to just react to the other person. You can choose to interact with them and with what they do and say in ways that can defuse the anger and fear for both of you.

CHANGE YOUR FOOTWORK, CHANGE THE DANCE

It also helps to understand that all interactions are like dances. We all tend to participate in certain habitual patterns, especially with the people we work and live with on a daily basis. The music (situations) may change somewhat, but the steps (reactions) remain essentially the same.

This means that when we do or say something, the other person involved tends to respond in an habitual way. We then respond to their response in our usual manner. The other person, in turn, responds to our response, and so on, and the dance is under way.

If your observer is out, you can begin to recognize the familiar set of steps as they begin. In this case, as in all others, knowledge is power. The knowledge that you are about to repeat the same old pattern gives you the power to do something different. You are not obligated to continue the pattern, unless you choose to do that. All it takes is for one person to change his or her footwork, and the dance changes. The same pattern *cannot* be maintained, if one "dancer" no longer follows the same steps.

How do you change your footwork? You do it by changing your responses to the other person's behavior. If your usual response to an habitual interaction has been to get upset, then by not getting upset you have immediately changed that particular pattern. The other person involved cannot maintain his or her old way of responding for very long if *your* response is different.

In fact, the only way we can ever change another person (or even have the right to try to change them) is by changing ourselves.

When we change our own responses to what's going on, the other person *has* to change, at least as far as their interaction with us is concerned. To continue repeating a familiar pattern, each person involved has to keep producing the same behaviors. Your refusal to maintain the old pattern means that the other person has no choice but to change his or her responses.

Be prepared, however, for a period of adjustment to the new pattern. You, yourself, may feel uncomfortable for a while, especially in the face of the other person's frustration and confusion at your breaking the pattern. Your "dance partner" may, in fact, be quite upset at first, because the familiar behaviors are no longer there. If you hold firm, however, a new, healthier pattern can emerge. Eventually everyone will feel happier.

To better understand how all this works, consider the following scenario:

Josh comes home from school in a bad mood. His mother, who has had a frustrating day of her own and wants a peaceful evening, asks, "What's wrong? Why are you so grouchy?"

Josh, who immediately feels attacked by being labeled "grouchy", replies, "Because Mr. Smith is a jerk."

"How many times have I told you not to call someone else, especially a teacher, a jerk!" snaps his mother, who fears that her son will never learn, or just wants to aggravate her.

"Why do you even ask me what's wrong?" Josh shouts. "You don't care about me. You always take the teacher's side, anyway!"

It doesn't require much imagination to see where this conversation is headed. Neither Josh nor his mother is really listening to what the other is saying. They are both caught in an old, unpleasantly familiar "dance" which invariably leads to misunderstanding and frustration on both sides.

Could this pattern be changed? What if Josh's mother decides that she no longer wants to continue the old way of interacting? If she has her observer out, she will be able to notice that her son is really distressed and unhappy.

She may then decide to ask Josh, "What's wrong? You seem really upset about something." This immediately defuses the original pattern by simply making an observation, instead of an accusation ("Why are you so grouchy?")

The likelihood is that Josh won't catch the change immediately. He may be so caught up in his anger and frustration, that he still refers to the teacher as a "jerk". This gives his mother a second opportunity to change her footwork.

"What did Mr. Smith do to make you call him that?" This indicates that Josh's mother doesn't like the term "jerk." At the same time, she lets Josh know that she understands that something he considers really bad must have happened for him to refer to Mr. Smith in this way.

At this point, Josh is free to let his mother know what actually took place, and they can begin to discuss what might be done to resolve the situation, or at least relieve Josh's angry feelings. As long as his mother keeps her observer out and does her best not to fall back into old patterns, she and Josh can make this particular "dance" a new, healthier one.

In this type of shift, where one participant works to be more understanding and helpful, it's likely that the other person will accept the difference gladly. However, if the pattern being changed involves one "dancer" no longer allowing him or herself to be abused in some way, the change may come as a shock and be resisted, at least at first.

For example:

Every time Martha visited her widowed mother, she allowed herself to be talked into doing all sorts of things she really didn't have time for or want to do. She ran errands, took her mother's car in to be serviced, even fixed lunch for her mother and several bridge club friends once a month. If she tried to protest that she didn't have the time, her mother sighed and made remarks designed to cause Martha to feel guilty and ungrateful. Martha always ended up feeling extremely angry and resentful, both at her mother and at herself.

Finally, Martha began to realize that if she ever wanted to have any respect for herself, she would have to make up her mind what she was willing to do for her mother, and what she was not willing to do. The next time her mother called to remind her that the bridge club met in a few days, Martha told her that she was busy and couldn't cook the luncheon. Her mother pulled out all the stops and did her best to coax Martha into keeping to the old pattern. When that didn't work, she began to attack Martha as a bad, selfish daughter who thought only of her own pleasure. Martha held firm. Finally, her mother hung up in a rage and didn't speak to her for a week. Martha, even though she was tempted to call and smooth things over, held to her decision.

Eventually her mother called and asked if Martha would take her to the mall. Since Martha knew her mother was afraid to drive in heavy traffic, she agreed. Gradually, over a period of several weeks, Martha created a new pattern of interaction between herself and her mother. Both of them ended up liking themselves and each other much better than they ever had before.

Changing old, familiar patterns usually isn't easy. It requires making a decision and then sticking to that decision, regardless of what the other "dancers" do or say.

CHANGE IS ALSO A FORM OF RETRAINING

As soon as we interact with other people, we train them to look at us in a certain way. They basically see us as we present ourselves to them. If we present ourselves as decisive and courageous, others view us this way. If we present ourselves as meek and "wimpy", they see us like that. Soon they expect us to always stay the way we've originally trained them to be aware of us. The only way to change our patterns of interaction is to take responsibility for retraining the people around us. By doing so, we make them see us in a different way, even though the change may cause some discomfort for a while.

Josh's mother and Martha both involved themselves in a retraining program. And they not only retrained the other people involved in their respective "dances". They retrained themselves, as well. *They began to view themselves differently, because of the different patterns they were creating*

YOUR FOCUS MAKES YOUR LIFE WHAT IT IS

You can see from all this that *where you put your focus truly makes your life what it becomes for you.* If you focus on yourself as being only who you have been in the past, that's how you'll remain. Other people will also see you in that same way, and you'll continue to repeat the same old patterns, healthy or otherwise.

If you usually focus outwardly into the drama we think of as daily life, you probably forget that "reality" is not always what it seems. Getting caught in the drama keeps you trapped in appearances. This often makes it impossible for you to even remember that you *can* shift your focus, change your mental sheets, and create a new reality for yourself.

If you put your focus where it does the most good, you turn it away from the outer drama and toward that deep, inner core of yourself which is your Source connection.

Putting your focus where it does the most good allows you to avoid being caught up in the drama. It helps you be an observer, as well as a participant, so you can be "in the world, but not of it". Putting your focus where it does the most good lets you open new doors and change unhealthy patterns to healthy ones.

A RECONNECTION MEDITATION

"It's easy to tell me to put my focus where it does the most good," you may say, "but exactly how do I do that?" One simple way to help yourself accomplish this and to also enhance your sense of connection to your inner core, the Source energy, is to practice the following meditation for a few minutes once or twice a day.

If you can, sit or lie down comfortably in a quiet place. Close your eyes and begin to pay attention to your breathing. As you inhale, say to yourself (either silently or aloud), "Dear Source (or "Dear God", or whatever form of address feels right to you). And as you exhale, say, "I turn everything over to You."

Just repeat that statement over and over, inhaling and exhaling. With each breath you breathe out, let yourself feel your tension and worries flowing away. With each breath you take in, feel peacefulness filling you. You'll begin to notice that your body relaxes and releases its tightness, as you breathe out all your negative feelings (anger, fear, guilt, resentment, etc.). Be willing to let go of your negative feelings for this short time. Understand that the Source knows how to deal with them much better than you do.

Since nature abhors a vacuum, removing your negatives means that the "emptiness" left behind will automatically be filled by something else. And because negativity is actually a form of addiction, the tendency is to allow other negative thoughts and feelings to take the place of the ones you've just released. In order to keep this from happening, you'll want to replace the negatives you're turning over to the Source with something positive.

So, as you continue to inhale, allow the Source love and healing to take the place of the negative feelings you're releasing as you exhale. Feel, see, imagine this Source love flowing into you as a beautiful, soft light. Let yourself be filled with this healing light.

This meditation can also prevent you from getting sucked back into the outer drama. If you begin to notice your focus slipping away from its inner center point, take a couple of minutes to breathe out the stressful feelings and breathe in peacefulness. You'll soon feel the negativity breaking up and melting away.

It's much easier to choose happiness when you keep your focus anchored in that inner center point, where it does you and everyone around you the most good. In the next chapter we'll discuss how to begin creating your new, happier life by asking for what you wish in ways that allow your free will to work for you, instead of against you.

REMINDERS FROM CHAPTER 3

1. Choose to make your focus more inward than outward, but go past your own emotions to a deeper place inside yourself, a place connected to the God/Source part within you.
2. By turning your focus toward this inner connection, you access a solid, unchanging core of good within yourself. This is putting your focus where it does the most good.
3. A focus lock is what happens when you get fixated on the way things seem at the moment. This keeps you from realizing that your view of a situation is only one of many possible views.
4. One way to break a focus lock is to remember to be an observer, as well as a participant.
5. Interactions are like dances. If you change your footwork (responses), the dance has to change.
6. The only way you can change another person is by changing yourself.
7. It's much easier to choose happiness when you keep your focus anchored to that Inner center point, where it does you and everyone around you the most good.

CHAPTER 4

STEP TWO:
ASK FOR WHAT YOU WISH, BUT ASK
WITHOUT DEMAND

"Realizing I don't have to do it all myself is a big relief."

EVERYONE HAS A "SPLIT PERSONALITY"

This doesn't mean we're all crazy, that something is wrong with us. It's simply a way of explaining what is sometimes referred to as our human "dual nature". Each one of us is made up of two basic parts. The first is that essential part which exists beyond what you see when you look in the mirror. This part is your true beingness, your soul, your Higher Self, which existed before you were born into this life and which will continue to exist after your body dies.

When you were born, this unique essential self, or soul part, enmeshed itself in the physical structure which is your body. When it did this, the second part of yourself came into being. This second part, your ego self, is also unique.

Scientists tell us that no two bodies (setting aside the idea of cloning) can ever be exactly the same. Your ego self is the combination of your own specific Higher Self and your genetically unique body. The joining of these two, body and spirit, has brought into being that unique and special creation which you think of as yourself.

Your ego self is, in its own way, as non-physical as your Higher Self, but there's a major difference: your ego self doesn't have the insight and the knowledge of how things work that your Higher Self possesses. Your ego self has to learn, sometimes with great effort, what your Higher Self already understands. This learning is gained through experience, and is heavily influenced by free will and choice.

CHOICE IS AN EXERCISE OF FREE WILL

One of the most important aspects of being human is that we have free will. Free will is a gift from the Source. It allows us to decide for ourselves what we will and will not do. And although free will *is* a gift, it is a gift somewhat like the traditional "double-edged sword," with which we can cut away something that hinders us, or whack off our own foot .

Free will gives us the ability and the right to determine our own actions and responses. It also places our Higher Self in the position of a backseat driver and puts our basically inexperienced ego self at the wheel. Because of free will, our more knowledgeable Higher Self is only allowed to whisper suggestions or warnings. Nó matter what our ego self decides to do, our Higher Self is not permitted to reach over and grab the wheel. That would be a violation of free will. Even if our ego self chooses to drive off a cliff, as it were, our Higher Self simply has to go along for the ride.

One of the things that becoming more connected to our inner core means is being able to make better use of our free will. We may sometimes be tempted to feel that we don't have free will, that we're victims of someone else's choices or of circumstances. What happens to us is, however, largely the result of the choices we've made through our free will. If we don't choose wisely, we usually don't like the results that grow out of our choices.

LET YOUR FREE WILL WORK *FOR* YOU, INSTEAD OF *AGAINST* YOU

When we choose beliefs and actions which help us, we let our free will work for us. When we choose those which harm or hinder us, we use our free will against ourselves. If we want to be happy, we must use our free will to make choices which benefit us.

One of our biggest challenges is making choices which are going to bring us results we'll truly want, instead of just choosing to follow what seems to be the easiest route.

We human beings tend to take any shortcut we can. We also try to avoid things we judge as "bad" or "uncomfortable". Problems arise, however, when we base our actions solely on taking shortcuts or on trying to keep ourselves from experiencing what we perceive as discomfort. This encourages us to act without considering the underlying circumstances, values or lessons of a situation. It causes our choices to be governed not by understanding and foresight, but by the desire to avoid immediate unpleasantness.

When we choose in this way, we use our free will against ourselves. Corner-cutting entices us to set aside what we know in our hearts is the appropriate way to do things. It also causes us to make spur-of-the-moment or nearsighted decisions. Then we feel upset because things haven't worked out as we wanted or expected.

To avoid such discomfort we must accept responsibility for our free will. We must use that free will to tap into the Source guidance that's always available within us. We receive this guidance through our Higher Self, which has far more information than our ego self can ever have.

When we ignore the information our Higher Self can give us, it's like refusing to look at a road map while traveling through rough or unfamiliar territory.

IN ORDER TO RECEIVE, WE HAVE TO ASK FOR WHAT WE WANT

Since the Source has given us free will and won't tamper with that gift, we can't expect to receive something we haven't asked for. This is the basis for Step Two: *Ask for what you want, but ask without demand.*

You may have heard the comment that we don't need to ask, since God can read our minds and knows what we want before we request it. God (the Source) does indeed know what we wish. But the Source isn't free to act on our behalf unless we give permission by asking. To force on us something we haven't asked for would be a violation of our free will. Therefore, it's essential to ask for what you wish.

ASK WITHOUT DEMAND

It's also important to avoid making your request in the form of a demand, because *a demand instantly creates a block*. When you make your request into a demand, you are asserting your free will and using it against yourself. It's like saying to the Source, "Give me what I'm asking for in this one specific way. Nothing else is acceptable. *I* know what's best for me, and my way is the only one I'm willing to consider!" When you do this, you force the Source to withdraw and allow you to take over. It does this to honor your free will, which you are now expressing as your determination to control the situation.

If you've thought in the past that God (the Source) has ignored or denied your requests, think again. You may have actually been blocking the Source's ability to help you by making demands instead of requests. **Remember: a demand is a block.**

HOW TO ASK WITHOUT DEMAND

There are two parts to any request. The first part deals with *substance, or what you want to receive*. The second part deals with *time, or when you receive it*. *Substance*, or what you want to receive, also has two parts. The first has to do with recognizing a problem and seeing, let's say, two possible

42

solutions. The way most of us tend to ask in a case like this is to say something like, "Here's my problem. I see these two possible solutions. Please show me which is the right one."

This may seem reasonable and polite (after all, you did say "please"). However, asking like this instantly generates more problems.

First, you are *demanding* the better of the only two solutions you can see. This creates an immediate block. Second, you are implying that you know everything there is to know about the situation and that these are the only two possible ways of dealing with it. In reality, there may be five, six, or even ten other possible solutions to your problem, all at the moment just beyond your present awareness. One of these may be the very best that you could find, much better than either of the two of which you *are* aware.

If you demand one of the two solutions you *are* aware of, you will probably never learn about the existence of the other possible solutions. In addition, your demand makes it difficult for the Source to easily give you even the better of the two you do know about.

ASK SO THAT YOU MAY RECEIVE

How, then, do you ask for what you want, so that you don't create a block?

Instead of demanding, say something like this: "Here's my problem. I see these two possible solutions. If one of them is what's best for me, I ask to receive it. If, however, there's something even better for me, please bring me that."

This immediately removes the block of demand. The Source is now free to reach beyond the present awareness, if that's what's needed, to choose the best possible solution. It is also free to present this solution to you in the very best way, at exactly the right moment.

The second part of asking without demand in terms of substance deals with your belief that *you* know what is best for you. Actually, in human terms, you usually do know better than anyone else what is right for you. But in ultimate terms, this may not be the case, because we're all blocked by two things: first, by our emotional involvement in our own lives and second, by the fact that our human consciousness is limited.

The human tendency is to say, "This is the deepest desire of my heart. If only I had this (relationship, job, money, situation), everything would be wonderful!" We're constantly urged to "know what you want and go for it." So we push and push until we finally reach our goal. Then we may find we don't want it after all, because of hidden factors which show themselves only after we achieve it.

Believing that you know what's best for you may lead you to state your request in the form of a demand. It's important to be aware that even if what you want actually *is* what's best for you, your demand will act as a block to keep you from receiving it fully or easily. You can see, then, that it's better to ask for what you wish as a preference, even if you can't conceive that anything different could possibly be better.

Keeping this in mind, you might want to word your request something like this: "Here is what I think I want. This is what I believe would be best for me. If that's true, I ask to receive it. But if something else would be better and make me happier, I'm willing to receive that."

This way you can't lose. If what you believe is best really is best, you'll receive it as quickly and easily as possible. If, on the other hand, it's not what will make you happiest, you'll receive, instead, what will. This protects you from your own possible lack of good judgment.

"I WANT WHAT I WANT WHEN I WANT IT!"

The second area to consider when you make a request of the Source is that of *time*, or *when* you'll receive what you ask for.

Let's assume that you're willing to ask without demand for what you want. ("Please bring me whatever is best for me.") Then you add, "But I need it *now!*" This, of course, is another demand, this one in terms of time, or *when* you'll receive what you're requesting.

It's possible that what's best for you can't be properly orchestrated by the Source for a week, six weeks, even six months. You have no way of knowing how long the process needs to take. The Source does know, however. The Source has no blockages of any kind and will, if allowed, bring you what's best at exactly the right moment.

BUT I HAVE A DEADLINE TO MEET!

A major difficulty can arise when you believe you must have an answer, a solution, by a certain time. It's important to understand that when you're truly asking without demand, a deadline may pass, but it won't mean what you thought it would. The process will continue to move on and, when the time is right, you'll be presented with what is truly best for you.

A reminder: "what is truly best for you" means just that— good that you will recognize as good, happiness that you will know is, indeed, happiness. Remember that your Partner in this business of life, the Source, is on *your* side. It knows what will make you happiest and will give it to you, if you give your permission and don't get your free will in the way.

One of your most important tasks is to learn that you can do only your share of the business, your fifteen per cent. The other eighty-five per cent is your Partner's share. Meddling in it only gums up the works.

THE PERFECT CAR

Even though she really couldn't afford it, Janet needed a new car. Each morning she asked for just the right car to be brought to her. She began looking, and found what she considered the perfect car. She put a down payment on it and applied for a loan through her credit union.

"One bizarre thing after another kept happening with the paperwork," Janet said, shaking her head. "Even the people at the bank were confused by the strange chain of events. The thirty days I had to get the deal together came and went, and the dealership couldn't wait any longer. They sold my "perfect" car to somebody else! I was really upset."

Despite her disappointment, Janet kept applying the second Step. She also worked extra hard with the third and fifth Steps, letting go of her frustration and making an effort not to judge what was going on. She continued to ask each morning for the right car to appear. Two weeks later, the husband of the woman Janet worked for said that he had just bought a new car and would sell his old one to her, if she wanted it. No down payment would be necessary, and Janet could work off the price of the car.

"It was much cheaper than the one I had picked out earlier, and a much better car," Janet smiled. "That was six years and 150,000 miles ago, and the car is still going strong. I couldn't see the whole picture myself. I just had to keep trusting that the Source would bring me what I needed, and It did! The hardest part was preventing myself from demanding that things be the way *I* thought they should be, instead of letting the Source take care of what really needed to be done, at just the right time."

ASKING WITHOUT DEMAND REQUIRES TRUST

The biggest difficulty in asking without demand is being afraid that if you say you'll accept whatever the Source decides is best for you, you won't get what you want.

When we make up our minds that we want something, we really *want* it. It seems impossible to believe that anything else could be as good, let alone better! Even thinking about saying "I'm willing to accept what the Source decides is best for me" seems scary. There's an almost superstitious feeling that making such a statement will automatically cancel out the possibility of receiving what we really want.

This misunderstanding about the process of asking without demand actually has lack of faith at its root. This means that we don't really trust the Source to bring us what will truly make us happy. And we not only fear that we won't get what we want. We're also afraid that what we *do* receive will be something we *don't* want.

We don't really have faith that what the Source sees as best for us will make us the happiest we can be. Part of this mistrust stems from the fear that "Thy will be done" means that God is going to do something inscrutable (and definitely not preferred) and we'll just have to bear up under it because it's God's will. In fact, practically every time someone remarks that something "must be God's will", they're talking about a situation no one in his or her right mind would want.

But isn't it possible that the Source wants *good* things for us, happy things?

Why do we have to assume that "God's will" is always the pits? It doesn't say much about our opinion of God, does it? Or God's opinion of us. What if God, the Source, is really on *our* side? What if "Thy will be done," could be said with excited anticipation, instead of resignation? Granted, sometimes the path to what really makes us happiest may have some rocky spots, some potholes. Most worthwhile goals require some effort to reach.

According to all the most knowledgeable teachers, difficulties and mistakes are how we learn. If we want to reach our goal (happiness), we do need to be willing to travel the road that will take us there. Just because it isn't always a well-paved superhighway doesn't mean the trip isn't worth while. The important thing is to have faith, to trust our partner, the Source, that everything which is taking place is part of a journey which will bring us to a place we truly enjoy.

TO TRUST OR NOT TO TRUST,
THAT IS THE QUESTION

Think carefully about what it means to trust or not to trust. You'll soon see that not only is there a great contrast in attitude between the two, but there's also a tremendous and far-reaching difference in results. .

When we choose *not* to trust the Source and Its ability (and willingness) to give us what we truly want, we make it very difficult for our Partner to help us. This is because demand isn't the only block to receiving. Lack of faith, or doubt, creates just as potent a block. So does hope.

In fact, hope is actually a form of doubt. Faith says you're willing to believe that everything is working for your benefit, even if, at the moment, you can't see that happening. Hope says you would like to believe this is so, but maybe it isn't. Faith and hope make very poor bedfellows. In fact, hope is only a step away from doubt, and doubt always breeds worry.**YOU CAN EITHER WORRY, OR YOU CAN HAVE FAITH, BUT YOU CAN'T DO BOTH AT THE SAME TIME.**

Faith and worry cancel each other out. If you're worrying, you don't have faith. And if you have faith, there's no need to worry.

If having faith is a problem, don't make this another thing to worry about. The Source understands that, being human, we can't be perfect. **In fact, to be human and to be perfect is a contradiction in terms**. No one can do it, and the Source doesn't expect perfection from us. All It asks of us is the willingness to work at our fifteen per cent (which means doing what keeps us connected to the Source energy), so that It can take care of the other eighty-five percent.

In fact, it's even all right to *pretend* faith, if you can't genuinely feel it.

"FAKE IT 'TILL YOU MAKE IT," IF YOU NEED TO

Pretending faith means being willing to practice the Six Steps, or whatever else you decide is useful, in order to continue giving the Source permission to help you. Faith, even pretended faith, keeps the process working.

Pretending faith also means that you ask *believing,* even if you allow yourself to believe only for the moment that you make the request. Doing your part in this way gives your Partner, the Source, continuing permission to help you in every possible way. And eventually you'll begin to see results which will generate genuine faith.

Pretending faith also allows you to avoid the pitfalls created by lack of trust. There are several of these pitfalls, all of them unpleasant. One immediate pitfall is feeling unhappy and disgruntled because life never seems to give you what you want. Another is cutting yourself off from your inner Source guidance. Lack of trust also makes it difficult, if not impossible, for the Source to help you in a truly effective way.

YOU CAN'T LOSE BY CHOOSING TO HAVE FAITH

You can see that choosing to have faith, even pretended faith, opens up all sorts of opportunities for the Source to help you. In contrast, not trusting, not choosing faith, is certain to lead to discomfort. It cuts you off from the Source's ability to help you and forces you to work on trying to make your life happy with only a fifteen per cent chance of succeeding. Choosing to have faith, on the other hand, puts you in a position where you can't lose.

Let's assume that you'd *like* to believe in the Source and its ability and willingness to bring you what will make you happy.

You aren't quite sure, however, based on past experience, that you're justified in doing this.

If you choose not to do it, not to have faith, not to trust, you need to understand that you are cutting off any opportunity that might exist for that help to be available to you. If, however, you choose to trust, to have faith in the Source, even though you may sometimes have to pretend that faith, your life immediately changes. That change may take place, to begin with, at a subtle, inner level. Eventually, however, it will work its way outward, creating definite positive effects in your daily experiences.

You can't lose by choosing to have faith and expressing that faith through following the Six Steps. Your life has no choice but to change for the better while you are applying these principles. You not only gain greater control; you also begin to attract to you the kinds of experiences which make you truly happy.

LEARN TO MIND YOUR PART OF YOUR BUSINESS AND LET THE SOURCE TAKE CARE OF THE REST

Remember that *what happens, how it happens, and when it happens is not your business*!

It's tempting to insist that things should be done when and in the way you think is best. But all this does is assert your free will in a way that forces your Partner, the Source, to withdraw from helping you. In a sense it's like saying, "Leave me alone. *I'm* doing it." The Source, out of respect for your free will, is obligated to do just that. That means you're stuck with trying to accomplish something you aren't equipped to undertake.

If you choose *for* yourself, instead of *against* yourself, you must make your requests into preferences, not demands, in terms of both substance and time. Then, after you state your preferences, you must be willing to let go of anything which would block the results. This means being willing to release your negative emotions to the Source.

REMINDERS FROM CHAPTER 4

1. Becoming more closely connected to your inner core means being able to make better use of your free will.
2. One of your biggest challenges is making choices which bring you the best possible results, instead of choosing to follow the easiest route.
3. It's essential to ask for what you wish, but to ask without demand. A demand creates a block.
4. You must choose to trust the Source to bring you what will make you truly happy.
5. You can either worry or you can have faith, but you can't do both at the same time.
6. It's all right to pretend faith until you develop genuine faith.

CHAPTER 5

STEP THREE:
LET GO OF YOUR NEGATIVE EMOTIONS

*"The best advice I got was to let go again and again,
realizing each time it would transform little by little."*

KEEP THE SUPPLY LINES OPEN

The third step in the Six-Step process, "let go of your negative emotions," is designed to keep the lines of supply open between you and the Source. If you choose to keep your negative feelings, they will, like silt, eventually clog up the channels through which your Partner delivers your good to you.

Holding on to your negative emotions also amounts to withdrawing your permission for the Source to help you. As we've noted earlier, it's like saying, "Go away and leave me alone. *I'm* doing this!" To honor your free will, the Source has to withdraw, and you're stuck trying to deal with your problems alone.

EMOTIONS ARE NEITHER GOOD NOR BAD

We tend to label our emotions as "good" or "bad." In reality they are simply what they are. In and of themselves, emotions are basically neutral. And no matter what kind of emotion you may experience, even rage or hatred, it has nothing to do with what kind of person you really are. We all continually experience all sorts of emotions.

"Negative" emotions are simply those feelings which cause us to be uncomfortable or unhappy. Emotions which fall into the negative category include anger, guilt, hatred, self-hatred, anxiety, and fear. Negative emotions are not by nature "bad" emotions, any more than positive emotions are automatically "good" ones. The results of holding on to either negative or positive emotions may, however, fall into these classifications.

It's important to understand that there is nothing wrong with feeling *any* emotion, no matter what it is. *It's what you do with it after you feel it that can create problems.*

As discussed in Chapter 1, we really have very little control over whether or not we *feel* an emotion. Emotions seem to just be there, often instantaneously. We do, however, have complete control over how we react to what we're feeling. *We always choose whether or not we'll keep an emotion.* And, if we keep it, we then choose what sort of action we'll follow as a result of holding on to it.

RELEASE EQUALS RELIEF

Take anger, for example. Everybody feels anger at one time or another. After you feel it, you can either hold on to your anger and let it eat you up, or you can acknowledge it and release it to your Partner, the Source. If you choose to turn it over, the Source will immediately begin to transform that anger into more useful qualities—love, healing, forgiveness, peace—whatever is better for you.

One way to release anger, or any negative emotion, is to visualize a bubble of light. Then place a symbol of your negative emotion in the bubble. (If a bubble of light doesn't suit you, create a visualization which does. One person I know places negative feelings in a tin can, shoots the can into outer space, and explodes it into the Light of the Source. Another one creates a basket which has a rope attached to it. When the rope is tugged, the basket, with its load of negatives, is pulled up into the Light. Let your own creativity find an image that fits your needs.)

If you like the image of the bubble of light, you can use it in the following manner. Let's say you're angry at your father.

Make a mental picture of your father and place that image in the bubble. Then imagine the bubble, with the image of your father in it, floating off into the Light of the Source. There it will be transformed into love, forgiveness, healing— whatever is better for you than the old feelings of anger. Keep in mind that what you're really letting go of is the emotion, not the image, or the person the image represents. So you're not turning over your father, but rather the anger you feel against him.

This particular example had real meaning for Cathy, who had a long history of being unable to lovingly communicate with her dad. By the time she was almost fifty, and he was in his late seventies, she began to despair of their differences ever being resolved. Finally, knowing she would be visiting him over a holiday period, she began to work hard at letting go of her anger and resentment against him, and of the fear that the barrier between them would never come down. Over and over again she put his image into a bubble of light and released it to the Source.

When she arrived at her parents' home, she found, to her surprise and delight, that her relationship with her father had shifted remarkably, without even the need to discuss it. "It was like a miracle," she said with tears in her eyes. "I was able to walk up and hug my dad and he seemed to sense the difference immediately. I now have, not just a comfortable feeling with him, but a closeness I never dreamed was possible."

Releasing your anger frees you from the pain of "getting into" it. If, however, you refuse to turn over your anger to the Source, you begin to expand it into all kinds of associated negative thoughts, memories, and feelings. These all feed upon each other and, in turn, upon you. You wind up with a negative focus lock which makes you and everyone around you miserable. It may even prompt you to behave in ways that you'll later regret.

DON'T LET TINY BUBBLES BECOME BIG PROBLEMS

Speaking of bubbles, you can also think of emotions and thoughts as being like the bubbles in a glass of champagne or soda water. If you watch them, you'll notice that these bubbles form, rise to the top, and pop. Thoughts and emotions, both negative and positive, form as effortlessly as bubbles. If you don't get into them, most will just as effortlessly "pop", or dissipate.

There's no point in worrying about the fact that you sometimes have negative thoughts and feelings. We all do—it's part of being human. The important thing is to realize that you're not obligated to keep these or expand them in any way. Those that don't just rise to the top and pop, you can consciously release to the Source. And the moment you're willing to turn over your negative thoughts and emotions to your Partner, in that very moment the Source begins to transform those negatives into positives.

LETTING GO IS SOMETIMES HARD TO DO

A word of advice: don't expect to turn over your negative emotions only once and have them stay with the Source permanently, at least not in the beginning. That just isn't human nature. You, like every other human being, get used to hauling around all sorts of unpleasant baggage; and when you first begin to let go of it, you often feel a bit strange, almost naked. It's hard to resist grabbing those negative feelings back, because you're so accustomed to carrying them. And even though taking them back is painful, it's familiar pain. But when you keep turning over your negatives to the Source again and again, you gradually begin to realize that what you assumed was nakedness is actually freedom!

For example, you may release your anger against your father, and five minutes later you think about him and feel ANGRY again. That's O.K. It doesn't mean you can't do it, or that the process doesn't work. What it does mean is that it *is* a process. And a process requires time and ongoing repetition to be effective.

Just know that every time you turn over a negative, the Source will work on transforming it for as long as you leave it there. So, when you experience that same negative emotion again (and you will, because you're human), don't be discouraged. Simply tell yourself, "Well, here it is again, so I must have taken it back. Let me turn it over to my Partner one more time." Do this every time you experience that particular emotion, even if there are a lot of "one more times" during any given day. Gradually you'll notice that the feeling is growing weaker, because you are always taking back less than you turned over the last time!

No matter what length of time you leave a negative with the Source, that much is able to be transformed into something positive. Whether you leave it a minute, an hour, or a day, it will be reduced by that much when you take it back. If you can only let a negative feeling go for one second, at least a second's worth will be transformed. This means that if you're willing to persist in releasing a specific negative as often as you feel it, over and over again, on an ongoing basis, you'll gradually just wear it out. One day you'll suddenly realize that you're no longer bothered by that particular negative emotion.

UNFORGIVENESS—THE CHAIN WHICH BINDS

Sometimes you may feel so furious at someone it seems almost impossible to find the willingness to let go of that anger. It's at those times, particularly, that you need to make every effort to turn over your negative emotions. The main reason for this is not because you'll have a more spiritual focus if you do, or that you'll be a bad person if you don't do it. The most important reason for letting the anger go is much more practical.

Anger is a chain which binds you to the person or situation against whom you feel it. You will drag them behind you for the rest of your life, unless you're willing to forgive them.

.

Forgiveness is the only thing which can dissolve the chain of anger. It also seems to be one of the hardest things a human being can do. This is mainly because of something we discussed in Chapter 1—"righteous" anger. In the case of forgiveness, righteous anger says, "Why should I forgive that so-and-so and let him/her off the hook? After all, he/she's the one who hurt me!" It's even tempting to believe that holding on to anger and resentment somehow validates our pain, even lessens it.

In reality, all that refusing to forgive accomplishes is to bind us to the person or event we feel so angry about. **In other words, holding on to our anger actually gives ongoing power over us to the very person we dislike so much.** Often that person is unaware of our feelings, or has forgotten the incident (which may make us even more angry). We, however, keep the pain fresh in our minds through our rage, resentment, even hatred.

And we are the ones who pay the price. Yes, we may have suffered in the past because of something that other person did or said. But refusing to let go of our anger, to forgive, condemns us to a life of constantly renewed suffering. And this suffering may not be only emotional. Recent studies indicate that stored anger often shows up physically as a variety of unpleasant illnesses.

WHAT FORGIVENESS REALLY MEANS

How can you forgive and not feel you've sold out or become a doormat? Mainly by understanding what forgiveness does and does not mean.

Forgiveness does not mean ever agreeing that what was said or done was good or acceptable. We don't ever have to condone what caused the pain.

Forgiveness also does not mean that we necessarily ever want anything further to do with the person we forgive. We may never want to see or hear from them again, and that's fine.

What forgiveness does mean is being willing to let go of our anger and resentment *for our own sake*.

Forgiveness means understanding that we forgive first of all for our own benefit, to free ourselves from the bondage of anger. This has virtually nothing to do with the other person! You don't ever have to tell them about your decision, or they may even be dead by the time you decide to forgive them. The person you forgive *will* benefit, of course, because you've withdrawn your negative feelings. However, the sense of freedom you'll experience will probably make it so you don't even care. (If you find it hard to let go of the idea of wanting to "get even," it's important to understand that the best way you can do this is to reclaim power over your own life. And this comes only through forgiveness.)

Don't worry about trying to "forgive and forget." We can't really forget. What we *can* do is forgive, so that we can remember without the pain. Only when we are willing to forgive are we able to let go of the pain and move forward, free of the terrible burden of anger.

As long as we refuse to lay it aside, this burden of anger taints every aspect of our lives and keeps us from being able to truly love. Until we forgive we can't really love ourselves, God, or anyone else. And don't forget; whatever applies to forgiving others also applies to the one who may be the hardest person of all to forgive—yourself! So, choose to lay aside your burden, to move forward, to love. Be willing to let go of the anger that binds you to the past.

Set yourself free—forgive!

RELEASE AND BE HEALTHY

Forgiveness is basically just the willingness to let our anger go, to give it to the Source, so it can be transformed into something more useful to us. Anger is a stimulating emotion. Some people use it like caffeine to keep them going. After a time, however, anger can take a devastating toll, with effects ranging from a sense of overwhelming burden, or obsession with being wronged, to such physical manifestations as chronic indigestion, arthritis, or even cancer. Letting go of anger is essential to both mental and physical good health. It goes without saying that spiritual health is also strongly influenced by forgiveness, or lack of it.

Betty had for several years done fairly heavy physical work, but when she injured her back moving a large piece of furniture, she had to leave her job.

"I committed myself to seriously releasing my negative emotions in the hope of getting rid of what had become a chronic back problem. The injury did heal tremendously well, but the most remarkable and unexpected result was the healing of my life. I found that letting go of my resentments and letting go of my worries were interconnected. Releasing my old resentments toward people or incidents from the past made it easier for me to release my worries.

"And when I began to worry less, it was much easier to let go of my anger. What resulted was a gradual deepening of an inner peace and a sense of well being I had never experienced before. Like a beautiful spiral, this process built on itself. All it took was my commitment to follow through with the discipline for thirty days!"

I'M SO MAD I COULD SCREAM!

Letting go of negative feelings does *not* mean repressing them. Repression is an attempt to deny or avoid the feelings. When you release your negative emotions, you have to first identify and acknowledge them, so that you *can* let them go. **You can't release anything you can't acknowledge.** If, for some reason, you feel that you just can't identify the specific emotions which are troubling you, you can still express a willingness to turn over any harmful feelings you have buried, whatever they may be.

If you feel you need to express your negative emotions in some way before you let them go, then by all means do that. But do it a way that won't be harmful to you or anyone else. If you're angry, admit the anger to yourself. Go in your room and scream, cry, punch a pillow. Or say out loud exactly what you want to tell the person against whom you feel the anger, as if they were in the room with you. If speaking your feelings aloud doesn't feel right to you, write the person a letter. You may or may not send it. You're really writing it for your own benefit. You can even bury or burn the finished product, in a sort of ceremony of closure. If you feel some direct action needs to be taken, then put that in motion, but do it *after* you relieve the immediate pressure, not in the heat of your rage. Once you've taken whatever action you feel is necessary, then be willing to let the anger go.

If you habitually feel you can't act without the push of your anger, you need to deal with that feeling. There are a number of ways to address this issue. You can use the breath meditation described in Chapter 3, practice the Six-Step method daily, work with a therapist— whatever feels right to you. Learn how to do what you know, at a deep level, is right for you, instead of what someone else, or "society", thinks you should do. Certainly you can listen to the suggestions others may make, but ultimately you must let your inner guidance, that information which emerges from your Source connection, lead you. Once you teach yourself to do that on a regular basis, you won't need anger to motivate you to action. Your behavior will, instead, flow out of your stable inner core, which is a place of strength, rather than being generated by unreliable negative feelings.

TAKING CARE OF NUMBER ONE

How can you take care of yourself and still stay kind, loving, and spiritually focused? First of all, remember that your inner guidance (your "gut feeling") always knows what's best for you. If you've lived very long, you've probably already learned from experience that when you go against your "gut", you usually regret it.

If you do something because you've allowed yourself to be talked into it against your inner guidance, it really isn't going to be good for anybody. This includes the person you allow to persuade you. **When you do what you know is wrong for you, it's also wrong for everyone involved.**

This is true because of what can be described as the "tainted gift" principle. Even though you may try to tell yourself that you're doing what you're doing to please the person who talked you into it, you're giving a "tainted gift." You're really doing it because you're afraid of their anger, or that they'll withdraw their love or friendship, or that they'll make you feel like a bad, selfish person if you don't do it. Behaving like this doesn't accomplish anything positive. Instead, you contaminate, or taint, the entire situation with your unavoidable anger and resentment against the person who persuaded you, as well as against yourself for giving in, when you knew you should stand firm.

This type of situation is also influenced by the third Basic Principle, which says that what you send out comes back multiplied. The entire atmosphere surrounding this situation and everyone involved is negatively affected. On the other hand, when you do what you know is right for you, you create a positive atmosphere. You haven't allowed someone else to influence you to act against your inner guidance, so you feel better about them, about the situation, and particularly about yourself. And you can be assured that **when you do what your inner guidance tells you is right for you, it is also right for everyone involved, whether or not they choose to understand that.**

TWO KEY QUESTIONS THAT HELP YOU
TAKE CARE OF YOURSELF

Do you have a habit of letting people persuade you to do what they want you to do, instead of what you know is right for you? If the answer to this is "yes," you might want to ask yourself these two key questions when deciding whether or not to do something. The answers will help you make a decision which will allow you to take care of your own needs.

1. **Do I want to do it?**
   If the answer is "No," then you don't even need to ask the second question.
   If the answer is "Yes," then ask yourself:

2. **If I want to do it, can I do it without stressing myself?**
   If the answer is "Yes," then do it. If the answer is "No," don't do it. (If the answer is "No," and you do it anyway, you'll almost certainly regret it, since you'll be going against your inner guidance.)

If you momentarily forget you've decided to take care of yourself and automatically say you'll do what the other person wants, you can still ask yourself the questions afterwards. If your answers indicate that you've let yourself be talked into something that isn't right for you, you can call the person back and withdraw from the commitment. Just tell them that you shouldn't have given an answer until you checked a couple of things. And, having checked, you found you just couldn't do it. They may not like that response, but if you've made up your mind, and hold firm, they'll almost always accept your decision without much argument.

Or, if you feel it's essential to keep your word, determine that the next time you won't respond to a request until you've asked yourself the two key questions. It's always a good idea to answer any request by saying that you will think it over and let the other person know your decision later.

MAKING UP YOUR MIND MAKES THE DIFFERENCE

Making up your mind is crucial in order to get people to accept your decisions easily. If you haven't made up your mind, you'll waffle. When you say "I wish I could do it, but...," or "I'd like to, but I just don't believe I can..," that wishy-washy quality gives the other person a place to drive in a wedge. And once they get the wedge in, they'll eventually convince you to do what they want. But if you make up your mind that you know what's right for you and you're going to stick to it, the other person will soon sense that there's no use in arguing.

No waffling. Just saying something like "I can't do it; I'm sure you'll find someone who can," transmits the definite decision on your part that you're now taking care of yourself and doing what is right for you. It also tells the other person you're not open to discussion on the subject.

Often we let ourselves be talked into things because we're afraid that if we don't do what someone else wants us to, they won't love us any more. It's an absolute truth that if someone stops loving you because you aren't doing what they want you to do, they never really loved you in the first place.

YOU'RE SO SELFISH!

For those of us who grew up trying to please others, taking care of ourselves can seem difficult, if not impossible. It also may feel scary, because we fear that others will think we're being selfish and self-centered. (And when we're not doing what they want us to do, they may try to make us feel guilty by telling us this.)

Part of the problem has its roots in the way some of our religious teachings are interpreted. For example, in the New Testament, we are told to "Love your neighbor as yourself."

Unfortunately, that's often interpreted to mean "Love your neighbor (and everybody else) better than yourself, and if there's a crumb left over, *maybe* it's O.K. for you to have it." That's not what the passage says, however. What it does say is to love your neighbor *as* you love yourself. This implies that you have to love yourself *first*, in order to be able to love someone else in the same way!

SELF CARE IS *NOT* SELF-ISH

Taking care of yourself actually makes it easier for you to love others. When you do what needs to be done for yourself, you create an atmosphere of comfort and rightness. You are then free to do things for other people without resenting the fact that you're giving them time, effort, and attention which you need for yourself. Not only that, but when you exhaust and deplete yourself, you have no resources left to draw upon.

Taking care of yourself allows you to be *more* giving and loving. The more you give to yourself, the more you have to give to others. The more you do what needs to be done to make your own life peaceful and happy, the more you *want* to give. When you take care of yourself, you feel so wonderful, so loving, so happy, that you just want to open your arms and let all that flow out to others. You can't help sharing, because your contentment pours out of you effortlessly. You actually do *more* uncontaminated service in this way than you would if you ignored your own needs.

You also make available to others the greatest gift you could give, except for helping them reconnect to the Source. You offer them the gift of your own joy. And when they sense the love and happiness flowing out of you, they feel that if you've been able to accomplish this, maybe they can, too.

Learning to take care of yourself also helps you clear out any resistance to releasing your negative emotions. When you do what you know is right for you, you automatically begin to dissolve your anger, fear, resentment and guilt. Forgiveness becomes easy, because you no longer need or want to hold on to anything which might tarnish or destroy your happiness.

"LET GO AND LET GOD"

This has become a popular saying in the past few years, with good reason. Keeping old pain and negative emotions never benefits anyone. Instead, it clogs up the lines of supply between you and the Source. Letting go of your anger, fear, guilt and resentment opens up a treasure house of good. It relieves you of the burden of negativity. It allows the Source to fully help you run your life far better than you could ever manage alone.

In addition to the methods we've already discussed, a great way to release your negatives on a daily basis is to learn how to "send them up the pipe." The next chapter will show you exactly how to do this.

REMINDERS FROM CHAPTER 5

1. Negative feelings clog up the lines of supply between you and the Source.
2. There's nothing wrong with feeling any emotion. It's what you do with it after you have it that can create problems.
3. It's only human to take back what you turn over to the Source.
4. Each time you take back a negative, it's less than when you turned it over.
5. Anger is a chain. It binds you to the person or situation against whom you feel it.
6. Forgiveness means being willing to let go of your anger in order to free yourself from bondage.
7. You can't release anything you can't acknowledge.
8. When you do what you know is right for you, it's automatically right for everyone involved, whether or not they choose to understand this.
9. Taking care of your own needs actually makes it possible for you to give freely to others.

CHAPTER 6

SEND IT UP THE PIPE!

"My sense of being powerless was transformed into strength by learning to let go to the Source."

It's always easier to work with a concept when you can visualize it. In Chapter 5 we discussed the bubble of light as a means of letting go of your negative thoughts and feelings. Another useful visualization is the one you'll find on the next page—the pipes.

If you need a quick way of getting rid of what bothers you, just send it up the pipe. What pipe am I talking about? It's the short, L-shaped one you'll see in the diagram.

This short pipe and the other, longer, one together create the perfect recycling system. You send your negative emotions up the shorter of the two pipes, which delivers them to the Source. Those which you leave long enough to be transformed are then returned to you through the longer pipe as positives.

Notice that both pipes also extend down into yourself. This extension of the shorter pipe allows you to send to the Source any negatives you've been thinking or feeling. The horizontal part of the shorter pipe, which opens out of your forehead, sucks up all the negatives that come toward you from outside yourself. These include all the unpleasant, unkind, or scary things you see, read, or hear. You then send them up the vertical part of the "L" directly to the Source. The process is similar to what happens when you send a deposit to the bank teller in one of those plastic cylinders at the drive-through.

Once the Source has received these negative emotions, It begins to transform them into positives. It then returns these to you through the longer pipe coming in through the crown of your head. Notice that this pipe also extends down into yourself, so that you can be completely filled with this returning good. Think of this good as flowing all the way down from the top of your head to the soles of your feet. Once you are completely full, any extra positives are then free to flow out through your heart to others. **The pipes are, indeed, the ultimate recycling system. You send off your negatives and receive them back as positives.**

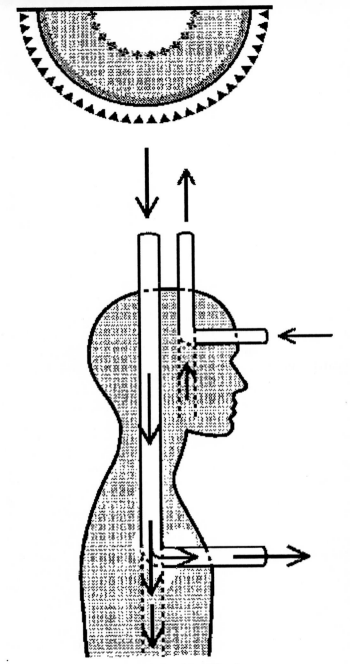

Drawing by Elsa Drake

70

DON'T OVERLOOK THE GOOD

Some people tend to use the shorter pipe and forget about the longer one. This means that they're focusing on sending off their negatives, which is essential, but they're forgetting to also focus on their returning good. You need to be as much aware of the good you're receiving as you are of the negatives you're releasing.

There may, for example, be lots of evidence of abundance opening up for you. But if you choose to see only what you *don't* have, you'll continue to create an atmosphere of need and lack. When you ignore your good, or refuse to recognize it because it isn't big enough, or just how you expected it to be, you convert the positives you're receiving into negatives.

In addition, if you keep ignoring your good when it shows up, you may begin to feel depressed. This makes it difficult for you to keep turning over your negatives. And the less you turn over, the less the Source is able to transform and return to you as positives. This means that the more you hold on to your negatives, the less good you are able to receive. It becomes a vicious circle.

So, accept with gratitude *all* manifestations of good, no matter how small or how unlike your expectations they may be. Recognize them as evidence that the process is working. Remember that the whole RECONNECTION process is designed to make your life happier and more fulfilled. Focusing on the good you're receiving helps you to recognize your increased happiness. This, in turn, continues to draw to you more and greater good.

In addition, noticing the good helps to keep you grounded in the present moment and out of the past and future, two areas which are, basically, none of your business. This, of course, means that they're your Partner's business, since only the Source has the ability to adequately take care of them, as you'll see in Chapter 7.

REMINDERS FROM CHAPTER 6

1. When you have a negative emotion, send it up the pipe!
2. The pipes are the ultimate recycling system. You send off negatives and get them back as positives.
3. Be equally aware of *both* pipes. It's just as important to acknowledge and receive the "good" as it is to let go of the "bad."

CHAPTER 7

STEP FOUR:
FOCUS IN THE MOMENT,
DOING WHAT COMES NEXT
AS IT'S PRESENTED TO YOU

"As I worked the steps, I found I was better able to truly enjoy the present moments of my life."

DO YOU BELIEVE IN TODAY, OR IN YESTERDAY?

Step Four says to focus in the present moment, doing what comes next as it's presented to you. This isn't always as easy as it may sound. Without even realizing it, many of us tend to direct a lot of our attention toward either the past or the future (or both), more than we do toward the present. Witness the fact that in one of the most popular songs ever written the singer, instead of enjoying his present moment, believes in and longs for "yesterday." No willingness to let go of the past or of negative feelings. No interest in making today as positive and happy as possible. In fact, the song, although beautiful, celebrates holding on to the pain of loss and unfulfilled expectations.

For some unknown reason we human beings have the ability to take a perverse pleasure in pain. In some ways, we actually enjoy suffering. We can, and often do, throw a "pity party" at the drop of the proverbial hat. When we do this it means, of course, that we're getting caught up in the drama of life. Getting sucked into that drama never leads to happiness. To be happy, you have to choose to keep your attention on the present. It's all too easy to let your focus slide back into the past, or creep forward into the future.

THE PAST AND THE FUTURE ARE FANTASIES

One thing that may help you keep your focus in the present is to realize that the past and the future are really both fantasies **The future is *always* a fantasy, because it never comes.** By the time it arrives, the future has become the present. Even if you could project yourself two hundred years ahead in a time capsule, the minute you opened the door and stepped out, it would no longer be the future. Instead, it would be the present.

The best that you, or anyone, can do with the future is to project and assume into it. Unfortunately, our future projections and assumptions are frequently negative. If you'll recall the third Basic Principle ("what you send out comes back multiplied") you'll see that negative projections are destined to bring back negative results. So, fearing the future helps to create the very thing you're afraid of, or a variation of it. It becomes a self fulfilling prophecy.

The past, in its own way, is also a fantasy. You always remember the past through the filter of your emotions. Since how you think and feel influences how you see things ("what you see is what you get"), you can't ever be absolutely certain that the way you remember an event is exactly how it took place Each of the other people who may have been involved in the incident will probably have a slightly (or more than slightly) different version of what happened. No one is "wrong," but no one is completely "right," either. In fact, there isn't any "right" or "wrong" involved. Each person will have experienced the event according to his or her own focus.

What a waste of time and energy it is to be bound to a past which may not even have happened exactly as you remember it If an event was painful, it's far more useful to acknowledge the pain and, if you feel you need to take some action about it, do that. Then, turn over to your Partner all the negative feelings attached to what happened. The Source can begin at once to transform them into something more positive and helpful to you This frees you to be focused in the present as fully and as enjoyably as possible.

THE ONLY TIME YOU EVER HAVE IS *NOW*

The third Step, turning over your negative emotions, makes it much easier for you to focus happily in the present moment. By letting go of those feelings, you no longer overlay your present moments with past anger and guilt, or future fears and anxieties. Why should you clutter the only time you really ever have, which is *now,* the present, with what might never take place, or may never have actually happened in just the way you remember?

You can't live a second ahead of or behind yourself. The only time you can really live is *now,* experiencing each present moment as it presents itself. When you try to live in the past and/or the future, you aren't really living. You're just existing, because you can't really *live* there. **Focusing away from the present into the future or the past means that you're actually cheating yourself out of your own life!**

This is why it's so important to focus in the moment, just doing what comes next, as it's presented to you. Of course, this doesn't mean you just sit and do nothing but inner work. You go about your everyday business, but with a difference. And the difference lies in your focus.

Instead of reacting to events from a past focus of anger and resentment or from a future focus of anxiety or fear, you now allow your Partner, the Source, to take care of these two areas and the emotions belonging to them. This is the only thing that really works, anyway, since you, as an ego self, a human being, have no way of knowing what's really involved under the surface of events.

Remember, you're limited mainly by two things. The first is the fact that you're naturally very emotionally involved in your own life. This can, and often does, cloud your judgment about what's going on at any given moment. The second limitation is that your human brain is limited, finite. Your mind is not finite, but your mind has to work through your brain, in order to function at this level of existence. The Source, on the other hand, has no limitations of any kind. It can and will select the very best for you and orchestrate all those themes so that you'll receive what ultimately will make you the happiest you can possibly be.

PUTTING YOUR PRESENT-MOMENT FOCUS TO WORK

How does this actually work? Let's say that you're looking for a job. What steps will you follow in order to stay in the present moment and let your Partner, the Source, take care of everything else?

First, turn your focus away from the drama that says times are difficult and jobs are hard to find. Next, ask (by preference, of course) that the very best job for you be opened up as soon as possible. Be sure to believe, at least in the moment of your request, that your Partner is already taking action on your behalf, even if you have to pretend that belief (see Chapter 4). Then let go of the anxieties and fears that nothing will happen. As you can see, you've now applied the first three Steps.

You do *not*, at this point, sit and wait for someone to knock on your door, begging you to come to work for them. You add Step 4, the Step we're discussing in this chapter, and do what comes next as it's presented to you. This means answering want ads, sending out résumés, going to interviews, following leads— in other words, doing whatever is appropriate and necessary.

But you do all these things knowing that your Partner is busy bringing the best possible job situation together for you, even though you may not immediately see what you consider the desired results.

If you feel your faith in the Source flagging, then remember to *pretend* faith long enough to continue letting go of any doubts and fears that the method isn't working. Remember that perfect faith is *not* demanded of you, only the willingness to persist in doing your share of the business. If you're willing to persist, you *will* be presented with the right job at exactly the right moment.

But faith, even pretended faith, is absolutely essential to keep the process working, because it is faith (real or pretended) that allows you to persist in doing your share of the business.

And doing your share is what gives your Partner the ongoing permission to continue to work in your behalf.

If the idea of pretending faith bothers you, think of it as willingness, determination, or commitment. However you label it, the important thing to remember is that **faith** (willingness, determination, commitment) **keeps you working at your share of the business.** And your share has to be taken care of first, or your Partner won't be free to take care of the rest! Also, as you persist in letting the process work for you, you'll begin to see results which will gradually transform your pretended faith into one that's genuine.

FAITH AND JOY

Maria has spent many years working with the Six Step Method and has applied it to a variety of situations.

"Letting the Source be in control of things isn't always easy. It means I have to really trust that It will do what's best for me. But only when I do that, when I trust, even if I have to pretend I'm trusting at first, does everything open up. It seems to me that true faith is being able to sort of stand aside and watch what's happening; not getting caught up in it, just doing what's presented for that day, without even thinking about the outcome.

"Also, joy is important—the joy of the moment. When you have faith and the joy that results from it, you are truly free."

THE SOURCE IS THE SOURCE OF YOUR SUPPLY

This is a truth which is easy to forget in times of stress or anxiety. If you've been having trouble finding a job, or have money worries because your present paycheck seems inadequate to meet your needs, remember this: **the source of your supply is *not* your job or your paycheck—it's your Partner, the Source.** Ask, believing that you'll receive, and your needs will be met. *How* they'll be met isn't your business. It's your Partner's business.

There's a wonderful story told about the Maharishi (founder of Transcendental Meditation) soon after he first came to this country. When he expressed his dream of building a university and meditation center, someone remarked that this would take a lot of money. "Where do you think that kind of money will come from?" the person asked. The Maharishi replied, "From where it is now." The university and center, and more, have since manifested, as the money came from where it was then to fulfill those dreams.

The Maharishi knew that where the money was located was not *his* business, but the Source's. *How* he would receive it also wasn't his concern. Staying connected so that he *could* receive it when the Source delivered it, was. You have to learn to trust, to have faith that your Partner can and, indeed, *is* taking care of the orchestration of the details. What those details are isn't your concern, unless they are presented to you as needing some input on your part.

If you demand, or even expect your needs to be met in a specific way, you're creating a block. This limits your good. The Source may provide for you in ways you'd never dream of—not just through a job, a raise, or a promotion, but through avenues which might not occur to you in your wildest dreams. Your part of the business is to ask, knowing that you *will* receive; to let go of the negatives; to do what comes next—in other words, to follow the Six Steps, to stay connected to the Source energy. If you do your part in a committed manner, you *will* receive what you need.

Just because you can't see where the funds or the help you want will come from doesn't mean that help isn't available. It just means that taking care of what you need is part of your Partner's eighty-five per cent of the business, instead of being part of your fifteen percent.

In fact, your fifteen per cent really consists of nothing more than doing what you need to do to stay connected to the Source, so that It is free to take care of the other eighty-five percent!

FIFTEEN PERCENT BRINGS RESULTS

My own most striking experience with understanding that the Source is the source of my supply came during a period where my finances were very low. It was shortly before Christmas, and I didn't even have the funds to buy my daughter a gift. I had, however, inherited a solitaire ring from an aunt. I had it appraised earlier and was told it was worth almost three thousand dollars. I decided I would sell the ring. I knew it was unlikely that I would get the appraised amount, but I hadn't expected problems finding a buyer. One prospective purchaser even said that her jeweler, on examining the ring, had claimed that it might not be a diamond, after all!

The original appraiser had moved to another city, so I mailed it to him to be reexamined. He sent it back with his report, but the shipment was lost en route! The shipping company informed me that their policy was either to replace the ring with one of equivalent value, or to pay half of its insured value. Since I only wanted to sell the ring, I asked that the money be sent to me. I was disappointed that I would only receive half of the insured value, but turned that negative emotion over as often as I felt it, and instead began to give thanks for the money which would soon be coming.

A few days later a check arrived for, incredibly, the full amount for which the ring had been insured. What an exciting Christmas gift! More important, what a wonderful manifestation of how the Source is, truly, the source of our supply and can bring what we need into our lives in remarkable ways, if we're just willing to do our fifteen percent.

A FULL TIME JOB

Once in a while someone says, "But I can't just live my life letting the Source do everything. Surely I have to take *some* responsibility!" This shows that they really haven't understood what partnership with the Source is all about. When you truly enter into that partnership you don't just sit, twiddling your toes, until something falls into your lap. You most definitely have work to accomplish, but the majority of it is *inner* (emotional and spiritual), rather than outer (physical) effort. It's also the hardest work you'll probably ever do.

You *have* to take care of your share of the business, your fifteen percent, so that your Partner has permission to take care of the rest. In fact, your share of the business is a full time job, if you're really serious about it. Not only do you have your everyday life to live, but you now have, in addition, the inner work of the Six Steps to pay attention to on a daily basis.

GUIDANCE COMES IN MANY WAYS

Part of that inner work is listening for whatever guidance you've been requesting. **If you don't listen for answers, there's no point in asking for information.** Guidance can come in a variety of ways. It can take the form of a dream, as something you read or hear that "clicks" in your mind and makes sense to you, as a gut feeling, or as a situation opening up unexpectedly. Any and all of these, as well as other subtle means, can give you needed guidance.

LISTEN TO YOUR GUT

If you're not used to asking for internal guidance, you can practice "hearing" it by asking, then asking again, and then again. Pay attention to what's going on inside you, in the sense of noticing if a "gut feeling" is beginning to grow. This is the most common way of receiving guidance. It's basically what people mean when they tell you to "go within" for your answers. A gut feeling is simply a growing sense of "yes, this is right," or "no, this isn't good for me."

Even though it usually takes a little while and builds gradually, eventually this sense of rightness (or wrongness) about an issue will begin to make itself obvious to you. If you'll think back on points of decision in your life, you'll probably realize that you've had some sort of gut response almost every time. If you followed that guidance, things usually worked out all right. If you went against your gut, you usually ended up wishing you hadn't. In fact, it's fairly safe to say that if your gut tells you one thing and someone else (no matter who) says something different, you'd better listen to your gut!

Sometimes guidance can come as a word, a sentence, or an image. Because these don't seem to have the strength of an intense gut impression, some people tend to feel uncertain about their validity. Is the information really guidance, or is it just imagination? One way to test it out is to request the guidance several times, and see if you keep getting the same answer. If you do, you can be pretty certain that what you're receiving is indeed guidance and not just what is sometimes called "ego static."

Pay attention to how your guidance "feels" to you internally. When information feels right, follow it. In the beginning you may have a mixed experience. Some "guidance" may turn out to be the expression of your own desires or someone else's influence. But gradually you'll build a sense of what is and what isn't genuine, what's guidance and what's interference. You just have to be willing to go through this necessary "training period" (as with any new skill) and have some patience with yourself while you're learning.

Sometimes people complain that they can't seem to get a clear response to their requests for direction. Believe it or not, failing to receive a definite answer can actually be another form of guidance. If, for example, you're trying to make a decision and, despite your requests you feel you can't sense a solid response, it usually means that something isn't right and you should just leave the whole thing alone, at least for the moment. Later, you may check again and find that your guidance on the issue has become clear.

Learning how to determine what is guidance and what isn't guidance *is* a skill. And, like any other skill, it takes practice to develop. But once you have developed it, you'll have an invaluable tool for directing your life more easily. Guidance is the Source's main response to your requests for help.

DREAM A LITTLE DREAM

Keep in mind that guidance also can come through information you receive in your dreams. Because of that, it pays to note down any vivid dreams you can recall as soon as you wake up. (If you don't jot them down immediately, they tend to fade away.) Dream messages can be very explicit, or they can be more subtle. If you're unaccustomed to interpreting your own dreams, you can get a dream book at the library. Better yet, focus on different aspects of the dream and ask yourself "What does this mean?" Notice the very first response that pops into your head. The first thought, image, or word that comes usually bypasses the thinking, analyzing process and makes it more likely that you'll receive the most useful answer to your question.

Getting your own information, rather than relying on someone else's, can be very important. Some dream symbols may be universal in their meaning, but many will be uniquely your own. Dreams often contain valuable information. They may deal with issues which face us in our waking lives, even though, in the dream, these issues are sometimes disguised as confusing or seemingly unrelated events.

LET YOUR GUIDANCE ANCHOR YOU IN THE PRESENT MOMENT

Guidance, whatever form it takes, points you toward the future in certain ways, yet at the same time fixes your attention in the present. When you listen for and follow your guidance you're directing your focus into the moment, doing what comes next as it's presented to you. Following your guidance and staying in the present moment as much as you can keeps you out of the pain of the past and away from the fear of the future. By focusing in the moment you're assured that you're living your life as fully as you possibly can. You're also doing your share of the business of life, which means that your Partner, the Source, is free to take care of the rest.

And now for the most crucial part of the Method—Step Five.

REMINDERS FROM CHAPTER 7

1. The past and the future are both fantasies.
2. You can only live in the present moment. Focusing on the past and the future cheats you out of your own life.
3. Do what's necessary, as it's presented to you, knowing that your Partner is taking care of the results.
4. Faith, even pretended faith, keeps the process functioning. This allows the Source to continue working on your behalf.
5. The Source is the source of your supply.
6. Guidance can come in many forms.
7. If you ask for guidance, it's important to listen for the answer.
8. Listening to your "gut" is more important than listening to the advice of others.

CHAPTER 8

STEP FIVE:
LET GO OF NEGATIVE JUDGMENT
AND YOUR RESISTANCE
TO WHAT'S HAPPENING

"I tried this and, to my surprise, things that used to frustrate me began to look interesting!"

HOW YOU JUDGE IS WHAT YOU GET

The fifth Step, letting go of negative judgment and your resistance to what's happening at the moment, is the most crucial Step of all. If you overlook this one, you actually cancel out all the other Steps of the Method. The success of Steps One through Four and of Step Six all hang on the persistent practice of Step Five.

Step Five is simple, but, as with the other Steps (which also are simple), it isn't always easy to accomplish. As mentioned earlier, "simple" and "easy" don't always mean the same thing, especially when they refer to making major changes in attitude and focus. I think the fifth Step isn't easy mainly because we human beings always want to judge everything that happens to us. And because we *are* human and addicted to drama, many of our judgments tend to be negative (negativity is undeniably dramatic). In addition, each time we judge negatively we understandably want to resist whatever we are judging in this way.

Why do we have such a hard time not judging people, events, and circumstances in a negative way? Probably because we tend to feel that everyone and everything, to be really O.K., has to believe and behave as we, ourselves, do. This fantasy (and it *is* a fantasy) gives us an illusion (and it *is* an illusion) of control. Therefore, when people and events don't fit the pattern we've decided is "right," we feel out of control and label them useless, uncooperative, stupid, or wrong.

Assessing and negatively judging people, events and circumstances is something we do all the time. We no sooner meet someone or experience something than we're busy deciding whether this person or that situation is good or bad. The problem is that ***it's impossible to be happy when you are judging negatively***. In addition, when you judge an action or an event as negative, you *make* it negative for yourself. How do you do that? Through your unconscious application of the first Basic Principle, which says that "what you see is what you get."

If you are to be happy, you have to be willing to let go of your negative assessment of what's happening and withdraw your resulting judgment from it. Instead of viewing a situation and complaining, "I don't like this, it isn't fair, I want it to go away," you must be willing to look squarely at it and say, "Well, I don't understand this and I certainly don't prefer it, but let me just watch it and see what it does." **This allows what appears to be negative to remain neutral.** Then, with the pressure of your resistance withdrawn, those particular circumstances can begin to shift into their proper places in the overall scheme, and the process of working things through to a happy conclusion can continue to move forward.

This is possible because, believe it or not, *events are basically neutral*. What is happening is simply what is happening. *You* are the one who assigns what's happening a value in relation to yourself. **If you decide that an action or event is negative, you make it negative, as far as you're concerned.** So, if you've been in the habit of judging events you don't prefer as negative, it's essential (difficult though it may seem) that you now react to them in a new way.

Take, for example, having a flat tire on the way to an important appointment. The usual reaction would be to become angry, frustrated and uptight because of the inconvenience and delay. If, however, you apply the fifth Step, you must react in a new way. To do this, you acknowledge and turn over your frustration and anger, and you now let it be O.K. (although definitely not preferred) that the tire is flat.

The reason underlying the need for this new attitude is found in the fourth Principle: "What you resist you lock in place." (And don't forget the fact that you can't fight what is. The tire definitely IS flat.) The more angry you become, the more you resist, and the more you resist, the worse matters become. If you resist, you will not only arrive late for your appointment, but you'll also be emotionally off balance and physically stressed out.

Acknowledging, then letting go of, your anger and resistance enables you to get the tire changed more efficiently, with a minimum of discomfort and wasted time. Allowing the flat tire to be a neutral, rather than a negative, event lets you keep your balance and move on to the next thing as quickly as possible. And who knows, that very flat tire may have changed the timing of your trip in a way that prevented you from becoming part of an accident in which you would have been involved, had you not been delayed. Stranger things have happened.

Letting go of negative judgment also makes a difference in personal situations. Let's say your life partner has said or done something which hurt your feelings or made you really angry. The immediate temptation is to assume that your partner's behavior was prompted by an actual desire to hurt you, or, at the very least, a total lack of consideration of your feelings. The next step in the judgment process is to decide that if he/she truly loved you, he/she would never have said or done such a thing. By the time you've reached this conclusion, you're not only actively resisting what happened, but you're also putting up a resistance to tapping into the love and caring which forms the basis of your relationship with this person who is so very important to you.

If your negative judgment and resistance continue, they may eventually destroy the relationship. Only when you are willing to let go of these negative reactions and move toward a connection in that loving space which is the core of any true partnership can you begin to discover the cause for what has taken place. Once you understand what prompted your partner's words or actions, you can more easily work together to reach a place where such painful interactions are no longer necessary. Or, if they do happen once in a while, you'll be better able to work through them quickly because you refuse to get caught up in judging negatively and resisting what's happening.

Another temptation when things apparently go wrong is to say something like, "How can this happen? I'm doing my best to work with the Source as my Partner and *this* certainly shouldn't be happening!" What is actually going on, of course, is that what's taking place is something you neither expected nor like, therefore you judge it to be negative. Sometimes it's really hard *not* to view an event or circumstance as negative, but it's still essential to do your best to let it remain neutral.

WHEN WHAT YOU DON'T WANT IS WHAT YOU'VE GOT

If you don't want to be stuck with a situation you dislike, it's essential to allow things to be what they are and let it be all right that they are that way at the moment, even though they are not expected or preferred. You certainly aren't required to prefer *any* circumstance or event, or to want it to continue. But fighting against what is will always be a losing battle. Resisting the fact that things are as they are creates a pressure—the pressure of your resistance—which locks them into place. Now you not only dislike what's going on—you're stuck with it!

You can see, then, that **the surest way to keep what you dislike is to resist it**. To make this clearer, think about what would happen if someone pushed you. Your first impulse would be to push back, in order to keep your balance. It's no different with events and circumstances. The pressure of your resistance to what's going on causes a counter-pressure to spring up. This counter-pressure pushes back against the event or circumstance you're resisting and locks it into place. You're now stuck with a locked-in negative and will continue to suffer with it as a part of your life as long as you persist in resisting it. In order for the situation to unlock and move beyond the surface appearance of negativity, you must be willing to let go of your resistance. This allows the counter-resistance to fall away, so that movement toward the best possible solution can open up and flow.

This is, of course, easier said than done. It's hard to let a situation be all right, when the overwhelming temptation is to shout, "But it *isn't* all right!" The key is to let things be all right the way they are *at the moment*, even though you would definitely prefer them to be otherwise. Letting things be all right as they are at the present moment doesn't mean that you want them to stay that way. It just means that you recognize and honor the fact that you can't fight what is and win. It's a matter of gracious acceptance of what can't be argued with. And it's a matter of understanding that the only way to change the "what is" you dislike so much is to withdraw your resistance from it.

In addition, you need to remember the importance of focus, that "what you see is what you get." Your willingness to view circumstances differently from the way they appear lets you see that no event, no "drama," is as solid and fixed as it appears to be. Remember to think of each event, each situation, as a circle, having a three hundred and sixty degree circumference. You, as a human being, are able to see, as if you were looking through a many-faceted lens, only one degree at a time. Turn the lens a click, and suddenly you see through a different facet, which lets you view the situation a little differently. And because you now see the situation differently, you experience it differently— which means that it literally *becomes* different for you.

PUT YOUR MONEY WHERE YOUR MOUTH IS

I, myself, had a very good example of how shifting focus works. A few years ago, while I was still working as a transformational therapist, everything suddenly seemed to "dry up." Only a few clients were coming, and some of those were unable to pay. There was also a recession in full swing. I began to panic, fearing I wouldn't be able to meet my financial obligations. As I let myself forget what I was teaching others, my financial situation became worse and worse.

Fortunately, it wasn't too long before I realized what I was doing, and that what I had here was a perfect opportunity to practice what I was always preaching to others—to stop negatively judging what was happening and to, quite literally, put my money where my mouth was, as the saying goes!

The first thing I did was to start seeing the situation as neutral, as simply how it was, and letting that be all right. Then began asking for what I needed. Next, I turned over my fears that I wouldn't actually get what I needed, or wouldn't get it in time. I began to view my situation as an opportunity to prove again that the Method works, instead of moaning about how awful it was that I wasn't earning enough to live on.

Soon money began to manifest in all sorts of unexpected ways. A few more clients did come, but not as many as I had hoped for. Instead, I received a demonstration of how the source of my supply is not my income, but the Source. I would receive a letter from a friend who knew nothing of my circumstances and in it would be a twenty dollar bill and a note saying, "I was just thinking of you and thought you might be able to use this." Clients who had outstanding bills for many months suddenly began to pay them. As I began to give thanks for these shifts in my financial condition and resolutely continued to let go of my fears about money, more clients began to make appointments until I once again had enough to take care of my obligations without straining.

One really striking example of how all this works happened one Saturday morning early on in my "dry" period. I badly needed an ironing board and a few other household items, but didn't feel I could afford to buy them new. Instead, I thought I would go to a yard sale and hope to find what I wanted at a reduced price. When I turned the ignition on my old car, it made a funny noise, but it finally started. I was too late to get to the original yard sale I'd planned to visit, because I had a ten o'clock appointment at the home of a client, so I went instead to one closer to her house.

I was browsing through the items available when a man I knew slightly approached me and asked if I would like to have coffee with him after we finished at the sale. He helped me load up the ironing board I'd found and drove off to the little restaurant, about half a block away, where we'd decided to meet for coffee. But when I turned the key in the ignition of my little junker, it went "click;" then nothing. The car was completely dead. My first temptation was to panic. I still had very little money, at this point. Although I did have an appointment to earn some in an hour, now I wouldn't even have the transportation to get there! I forced myself to take a deep breath. "O.K.," I said to the Source, "you take care of this, please. I'm going to have coffee."

My acquaintance asked why I arrived at the restaurant on foot (which he saw from his seat in the window). When I told him, he offered me the use of his car for the weekend, until mine could be repaired. "We're here to help each other," was his comment when I expressed my amazement that he'd do such a thing.

I took him home and then drove his car to my appointment. While there, I called the automobile club to have my car towed to the service station near my apartment which did all my repair work. They indicated it would be at least an hour before anyone could come, too close to the time the repair department would be closing, so that I'd almost certainly have to wait until Monday. Again, I made a real effort to turn over my frustration, and let it be O.K. that I probably wouldn't reach the service station in time. I drove my acquaintance's vehicle over to the yard sale parking area, so I could stand by my car and wait for the tow truck, aware that I might have to be there for at least an hour.

To my surprise (this was a day of surprises!), the tow truck pulled in right behind me. When we reached the service station, I found that the distance was exactly five miles, which meant I didn't have to pay any extra for the towing. Not only that, but the mechanic said that he knew I needed to have my car that day so, even though they closed at two, and it was now past noon, he'd try to get it done, which he did. When I picked up my car, I found a bill for sixty dollars which, of course, I didn't have. Again, I released my fear, discovered that I had a tiny bit of room on my Visa card, which just took the amount, and gave thanks for that.

When I reached my apartment, I opened my mail and discovered that there was a note from a friend in North Carolina. Inside was a check for, you guessed it, sixty dollars. I realized later that had I, at any point, become upset and refused to turn over my negative judgment and my fears about what was going on, I would almost certainly have brought the whole, incredible process to a halt. Instead, the entire day became an exceptional example to me of how letting go of judgment and resistance to what's happening really works.

HOW YOU VIEW THINGS
MAKES THEM WHAT THEY ARE FOR YOU

So, don't forget that your focus shapes your experience. **When a seemingly negative event takes place, it is essential to remind yourself, "How I view this makes it what it is for me."** It is your willingness to shift your focus so that you can view events as neutral, rather than as negative, that keeps them from becoming negative. And the less negative your focus remains, the sooner things can open up and shift for the better.

Understanding and accepting the principle of non-resistance (or at least being willing to work with it, even if you don't feel you can completely accept it) helps you to continue practicing the Six Steps on a daily basis, which is essential if they are to work. Remembering the importance of the fifth Step is also essential. If you don't apply Step Five to the negative-seeming situations you encounter, you not only lock those negative circumstances in place, but you also effectively cancel out the other five Steps.

Why is this? Because if you are negatively judging and resisting what's going on, you can't practice Steps One, Two, Three, Four and Six. When you judge and resist, you can't put your focus where it will do the most good. Instead, you're focusing on the fact that you don't like what's happening and assuming that it will produce negative results. You are no longer asking without demand, because now you're demanding that the situation be changed from the way it is at the moment to become what you assume would be better. You're not turning over your negative emotions, either. Rather, you're feeling angry, anxious, even fearful about what's going on. This keeps you out of the present moment, throwing you back into the past, where your anger and anxiety come from, and forward into the future, with your fear of unpleasant results.

Finally, refusing to let go of negative judgment and the resulting resistance prevents you from practicing the sixth Step, which reminds you to notice and give thanks for the good in your life. When you are focused on negatively judging and resisting events, how can you possibly pay attention to the good things life is offering you?

Let's take a closer look at this sixth Step and why it's so important to focus on the good happening around you, instead of getting sucked into the drama of what appears to be negative.

(If you're still having a hard time accepting Step Five, review the explanation of the fourth Basic Principle, near the end of Chapter Two.)

REMINDERS FROM CHAPTER 8

1. It is impossible to be happy when you are negatively judging people, events, or circumstances.
2. If you decide an event or circumstance is negative, you make it negative, as far as you are concerned.
3. In order to practice Step Five, you must be willing to stop judging negatively and resisting what is happening in your life.
4. Letting go of negative judgment of and resistance to what's happening allows events to remain neutral, instead of making them negative.
5. When you resist something, you lock it in place. In other words, the surest way to keep what you dislike is to resist it.
6. For every negative-seeming event which occurs in your life, remind yourself, "How I view this makes it what it is for me."
7. If you aren't willing to practice the fifth Step, you cancel out the other Steps of the Method. Step Five is the one on which all the others hang.

CHAPTER 9

STEP SIX:
NOTICE AND GIVE THANKS
FOR THE GOOD IN YOUR LIFE

"I've had to teach myself to focus on the positive things going on, instead of on the negative drama in my life. What a difference it makes!"

WHAT YOU "SEE" ON A REGULAR BASIS DEFINITELY INFLUENCES WHAT YOU GET

Here again, focus is the important thing. Remember that what you focus on is what you draw into your experience. Like truly does attract like, as the saying goes. So, if you want to have good things consistently showing up in your life, you have to pay attention to the good you receive and express your gratitude for it. Doing this creates a climate which allows you to receive even more good.

Keep in mind that you're not giving thanks for the good that comes your way because the Source needs that kind of attention from you. Feeling grateful is really for *your* benefit. "The attitude of gratitude," as some refer to it, is very important. Expressing your appreciation keeps you focused on the positive things that are happening in your life, instead of allowing your attention to be pulled into the negative-seeming dramas which sometimes appear.

It's also important that you don't make the mistake of thinking that "good" is necessarily the same as "big" or "dramatic." True, some positive events are outstanding and present themselves with a flourish. But what is good in your life can be as simple as the song of a bird, or the gentle touch of a loving hand. It can be as quiet as an understanding smile or the fresh-washed smell of the earth after rain.

If you are determined that good things can only come in big packages, you will consistently overlook many important, though modest, benefits. This will tend to cause you to feel that nothing, or very little, is going your way. On the other hand, noticing and feeling grateful for these smaller gifts sets your focus in a positive direction. And just as warmth, moisture and light in a greenhouse create the right growing conditions for plants, so the positive focus of noticing your good, no matter how small, and giving thanks for it creates a climate which makes it possible for even more and greater good to blossom in your life.

SPECIFIC EXPECTATIONS EQUAL DEMANDS

You also need to be aware that if you have specific ideas of how your good should show itself you are making demands of the Source, because specific expectations are actually just that—demands. Another problem with deciding that events should work out in a certain way in order to be good is that you'll tend to judge what happens as negative if it doesn't fit your expectations. And, if you do this, you'll almost certainly begin to resist what's going on, canceling out the fifth Step and, as a result, the entire Method (see Step Five, Chapter 8). In addition, you'll be tempted to overlook or deny the good that actually is occurring in your life, because it doesn't fit your expectation of what good *should* be. All of this creates a climate of dissatisfaction and lack of faith which may eventually lead you to believe that the Six Steps don't work and that your efforts are useless.

The way to avoid this dilemma is to set aside those specific expectations which can lead you to judge your good and perhaps deny it. Simply expect "good," in general, as much as possible, and look for that good in every event that takes place throughout each day. As you do this, you allow your awareness of good things happening to grow and expand. This keeps attracting further good and drawing it into your experience.

Expecting a more generalized good, instead of some specific one, doesn't mean you can't use visualization to help you attract what you desire, if you want to do that. Visualization has been shown to be very effective, when practiced with a strong focus and a belief in its ability to work. Picturing what you want is fine, as long as you make it a preference, not a demand. This means that you can create the image of what you would like, and see it moving into your experience, but you would want to add the rider, "This, or whatever is better for me." Making that statement as willingly as possible keeps your visualization from becoming a demand, which is important, because a demand will block the Source's ability to bring you what you're asking for. (Review Step Two, Chapter 4.)

Whether or not you visualize your preferences, try to be constantly aware of all the good, large or small, that is present in your life from day to day. Give thanks for it on a regular basis, either silently or aloud. Do your best to be thankful at the very moment that you notice something good taking place. This keeps you in a positive frame of mind. In addition, go back over your day at bedtime, doing your best to remember everything good that happened. You may be surprised to discover how much you've forgotten, either because you've overlooked it, or because you've overlaid your good with negatives.

List the day's good in your Notebook (see Chapter 11), or make a mental note of it, and express your gratitude, either silently or aloud. Next, make this list of good the focus you take into sleep with you. The focus that goes with you into the dream state is intensified there. If your focus is negative, you won't sleep well and your negative emotions will be just that much more difficult to dislodge in the morning. If your focus is positive, you will usually rest better, and the day will begin more pleasantly.

DREAM A USEFUL DREAM

Once in a while you may find yourself experiencing what seem to be unpleasant dreams, in spite of focusing on your good

97

as you fall asleep. If this happens, keep in mind that such dream usually reflect one or more of the following situations:

1. "Unpleasant" dreams may be expressions of tensions built up in the body and mind during the day which are releasing as your muscles relax.
2. "Unpleasant" dreams may be messages that there are specific negatives or related groups of negatives which you are finding difficult to leave with the Source.
3. "Unpleasant" dreams may be offering you an opportunity to work with issues which are difficult for you to surface or confront at the waking level.

Whatever the reason for what seem to be unpleasant o uncomfortable dreams, allow yourself to view these as tools yo can use to expand your understanding of your negative emotion: This expanded awareness helps you to more easily acknowledg and release these negatives to the Source, and also allows you t work on them through counseling, meditation, or whatever bes suits your needs.

The more willing you are to deal with your negative feelings the more quickly you can understand the "message" a difficul dream is bringing you. This also helps you to view such a drear as the Source's offering of good to you, instead of seeing it as failure on your part, or on the part of the Method.

Remember, the more you allow yourself to notice an give thanks for any and all good in your life, the more yo are able to receive even greater good on a regular basis.

You've now studied each of the Six Steps in individu: detail. Let's see how they all come together so that you ca create the happy life you truly want and deserve.

REMINDERS FROM CHAPTER 9

1. If you want to have good in your life, you must focus on all the good that happens for you. This creates a climate which allows you to receive even more good.
2. "Good" does not always equal "big" or "dramatic." It's important to express gratitude for *all* the good in your life, whether large or small.
3. Do your best to expect generalized good. Specific expectations act like demands and make it difficult for the Source to bring you what you want.
4. List, give thanks for, and focus on the good from each day before you go to sleep at night.
5. "Unpleasant" dreams can be viewed as gifts from the Source which help you to work on issues difficult to deal with.
6. The more you notice and give thanks for the good in your life, the more good you are able to receive.

CHAPTER 10

PUTTING IT ALL TOGETHER

"Working with the Source as my partner has given me faith
that everything in life happens for a reason,
even though I may not always know
what that reason is."

MAKE A COMMITMENT TO YOUR OWN HAPPINESS

As you've seen in this book, the Six Step Method is basically simple to understand. However, it isn't always easy to do. (Once again, "simple" and "easy" are not always the same thing.) It's not easy because it requires a commitment from you, a determination to work with the Method on a daily basis, even when you'd rather not bother to make the effort. In one sense, this commitment is to the Source. In the truest sense, however, it is a commitment to yourself and your own happiness.

You are the one who will benefit the most. It is your life which will be transformed, which will open up and begin to flow more easily. It is your growth and development which will be expanded. If you do make a commitment to work with the Six Steps, you will soon discover that they do work. The Source will not betray you or let you down. **But remember—you have to take care of *your* share of life's business first. If you don't do this, your Partner, the Source, won't be free to do Its part.**

What is your share of life's business? Once again, it is to:

1. **Put your focus where it does the most good.**
2. **Ask for what you wish, but ask without demand.**
3. **Let go of your negative emotions.**
4. **Focus in the moment, doing what comes next, as it's presented to you.**
5. **Let go of negative judgment and resistance to what's happening.**
6. **Notice and give thanks for the good in your life.**

This is the sum total of your share of life's business. Everything else is the business of your Partner, the Source.

THE IMPOSSIBLE DREAM

Keep in mind that **what happens, when it happens, an how it happens is *not* your business.** You have neither th knowledge nor the understanding to adequately deal with thes areas. Your Partner, on the other hand, is more than capable c taking care of this share of your life's business, as long as yo continue to give It permission to work and don't get in the wa by trying to take control of what you aren't equipped to handle.

Remember that it is a paradox, but only by turning ove control of your life to that part of yourself which knows exactl what to do with it (meaning your Partner, the Source) will yo ever really gain control. You can struggle your entire lifetime t be in control of everything, but achieving that is truly th impossible dream. We human beings like to think that, with little extra effort, we can direct our lives exactly as we choos We explain away the fact that this never really happens for an length of time by telling ourselves that we just didn't try har enough.

Only when we're willing to acknowledge that we simpl don't have the power or the skills to really run our lives we without help can we hope to gain the control we long for. Only when we're ready to share the work with our Partner do our lives begin to smooth out and bring us the happiness we want.

A REWARDING EXPERIMENT

Don't just take my word for it. Practice the Six Steps for a month or two, as an experiment, and see what they can do for you. (Just remember that it must be a *committed* experiment, not a once-in-a-while one.) By the time several weeks have passed, I'm certain you'll begin to see results which convince you that this partnership with the Source does, indeed, work and work well.

There isn't any doubt that, at least at first, it takes more effort to be happy than to allow yourself to be dissatisfied and miserable. You can be *un*happy by simply sitting and doing nothing, by being caught up and swept along in life's "drama." If, on the other hand, you've decided that you want to make happiness your goal, you'll have to be willing to put forth some extra effort.

The simplest way to do this is to determine that each day, for at least one month, you'll make practicing the Six Steps a top priority. In spite of all your good intentions, there will, of course, be times when you forget and fall back into old patterns. When this happens, apply the fifth Step and don't judge yourself negatively or start resisting the fact that you "backslid." Just turn over the mistake to the Source, and move on.

START THE DAY RIGHT

Do your best to begin your day by going over the Six Steps briefly in your mind. You might want to list them on a piece of paper which you can read as soon as you get out of bed (or even while you're still lying there in a relaxed state). Make a real effort to put your focus on the Source as your Partner, and your commitment to practice the Steps that day.

Next, write in your Six Step Notebook (see Chapter 11) all of your requests (preferred, not demanded, of course) and offer them to the Source. Then, list all the negative thoughts, feelings, etc., you're aware of holding in your mind and heart and do your very best to release them into the Source's healing Light. Now, you're as clear as possible, and ready to face the world.

During the day, make an effort to notice any negative feelings that come up and immediately turn them over. When things you don't prefer take place, immediately do your best to let go of your negative judgment about and resistance to them. Stay as focused in the present moment as you possibly can, dealing with whatever life presents to you in as positive a way as possible. Try not to drag old pains and angers out of the past, and stop yourself from projecting negatively into the future. Finally, let yourself be aware of every good thing possible, as soon as it happens, and express your gratitude for it.

When bedtime arrives, write down in your Notebook all the negatives you're still feeling, and turn each one over to the Source. Then make a final list of all the good things which have happened during the day, no matter how small, and focus on these as you fall asleep.

Simple, isn't it? But be sure you remember that any or all of the Steps are easy to overlook when you're pressured by the events of the day. Of course, forgetting once in a while is all right, too. It's very human to temporarily get caught up in old patterns. When this happens, don't beat yourself up about it. Acknowledge it, turn it over, and move on. And although practice doesn't really make perfect (no one can be perfect), it does make for improvement. The more you practice the Steps, the better you'll get at remembering to practice them. The important thing is to hold firm your commitment to keep working the Steps on a daily basis.

YOU HAVE NOTHING TO LOSE BUT YOUR PAIN

This rewarding experiment requires only your willingness to make the commitment to invest some time and energy in it daily. Keep in mind that "willingness" and "will" are two different things. You can't *will* yourself to carry out what you have committed to, but if you are *willing*, you can then use your will to hold that commitment firm. Your willingness to persist in applying the Six Steps each day will gradually help them to become second nature.

As this takes place, you will begin seeing results which increase your faith in the process which, in turn, will make it easier for you to continue practicing the Steps. This constantly strengthening circle of activity will gradually provide growing evidence that you are not alone—that you do, indeed, have a Partner who is both willing and able to help you. With this Partner's help, you will no longer need to struggle and strain. Instead, your life can become an exciting adventure that unfolds before you, as you walk into it. Happiness can become not just a goal, but a daily experience.

You have nothing to lose but your pain, and everything to gain. The choice is yours.

REMINDERS FROM CHAPTER 10

1. A commitment to practice the Six Steps is really a commitment to yourself and your own happiness.
2. You have to take care of your share of your life's business before the Source is free to take care of the rest.
3. Your share of life's business is, quite simply, the Six Steps.
4. What happens, when it happens, and how it happens is *not* your business.
5. Only when you turn over control of your life to the Source do you ever truly gain control.
6. A commitment to practice the Six Steps daily can result in happiness becoming a daily experience.

CHAPTER 11

YOUR SIX STEP NOTEBOOK

These pages will help you begin your thirty-day experiment of practicing the Six Steps in a committed way. The program is most effective, at least for the first month, if you actually keep a notebook on your desk or by your bed and write down your requests (preferences), negatives to release, and positives to remember.

THE THIRTY DAY PROGRAM

Each morning:
  (1) State your requests as preferences, instead of demands. Write each one down in your notebook.
  (2) List whatever negative emotions (fear, anger, self-hatred, etc.) you are dealing with and willingly turn them over to the Source.
  (3) Turn on your Pipes.

During each day:
  (1) Notice when you take back negatives you've already turned over, or when you take on new ones.
  (2) Release these negatives to the Source as soon as you become aware of them.
  (3) Remember to use the Bubble of Light and the Pipes.
  (4) Notice everything good that happens and express your gratitude to the Source.

Each evening:
- (1) List any negatives you feel you are still working with and release them to the Source.
- (2) Make a list of all the good things you can recall that happened during the day and give thanks for them.
- (3) Focus on these positives as you fall asleep.

After a week or two, you'll be able to see which negatives you have the most trouble releasing, as well as noticing more and more good entering your life. If the morning and evening lists look alike for awhile, don't be discouraged. It may take more than a month, but eventually you should find the negative lists getting shorter and the positive list growing longer. By the month's end, you should be seeing enough positive change in your life that you will be very willing to continue with the Six Steps. *However, do remember that you have to work every day, as a commitment to your own happiness, for the Method to be truly effective.*

Also keep in mind that practicing the Six Steps for thirty days is a beginning, a training period to help you integrate them into your life as a new set of habits. If you are to receive continuing, lasting results, you will want to make the Method a part of your daily experience. When you do, you will find that you have, indeed, transformed your life and given yourself the ongoing gift of lasting happiness.

.

SUGGESTED READING

1. Borysenko, Joan — *Guilt is the Teacher, Love is the Lesson*; *Power of the Mind to Heal*; and others
2. Carlson, Richard — *You Can Feel Good Again; Don't Sweat the Small Stuff (and It's All Small Stuff)*; and others
3. Chopra, Deepak — *Unconditional Life*; *Quantum Healing*; *The Seven Spiritual Laws of Success;* and others
4. Dyer, Wayne — *You'll See It When You Believe It; Real Magic; Transformation* (available on cassette); and others
5. Hay, Louise — *You Can Heal Your Life; 101 Ways to Happiness;* and others
6. Nhat Hanh, Thich — *Being Peace*; *Peace is Every Step*; and others
7. Ray, Michael and Myers, Rochelle — *Creativity in Business*
8. Zukav, Gary — *Seat of the Soul; Soul Stories;* and others

ABOUT THE AUTHOR

Barbara Goosen Shelby was born in Akron, Ohio. She has a Bachelor of Arts degree in Latin and Greek and a Master of Arts degree in archaeology, and has taught Latin at both the university and the secondary level.

A strong interest in emotional health and spiritual growth has led Barbara, over the past twenty-six years, to share the Six-Step Method with people seeking to improve their lives, including members of the mental health community, educators, spiritual leaders, and medical personnel. Barbara's work has reached as far as Canada, Germany and New Zealand.

Printed in the United States
778200001B

9 781585 007851